Ellen Thro

The NetWare Decoder

W9-CGV-261

A DICTIONARY OF TERMS AND COMMANDS

Covers NetWare

v. 2.2 and 3.11,

Portable NetWare

and NetWare Lite.

M&T BOOKS

The NetWare Decoder

A DICTIONARY OF TERMS AND COMMANDS

Covers NetWare

v. 2.2 and 3.11,

Portable NetWare

and NetWare Lite.

 M&T Books
A Division of M&T Publishing, Inc.
411 Borel Avenue
San Mateo, CA 94402

Limits of Liability and Disclaimer of Warranty
The Author and Publisher of this book have used their best efforts in preparing the book and the programs contained in it. These efforts include the development, research, and testing of the theories and programs to determine their effectiveness.

The Author and Publisher make no warranty of any kind, expressed or implied, with regard to these programs or the documentation contained in this book. The Author and Publisher shall not be liable in any event for incidental or consequential damages in connection with, or arising out of, the furnishing, performance, or use of these programs.

Library of Congress Cataloging-in-Publication Data

Thro, Ellen.
    The NetWare Decoder/by Ellen Thro
        p. cm.
    ISBN 1-55851-159-8 : $26.95
      1. Operating systems (Computers) 2. NetWare (Computer file) 3. Local area networks (Computer networks) I. NetWare decoder. II. Title
QA76.76.063T49 1992   91-44578
004.6'8--dc20   CIP

Project Editor: Tova Fliegel   **Cover Design:** Lauren Smith Design
Copy Editor: Linda Swain   **Layout:** Stacey Evans
Technical Reviewer: Steve Tolman

95   94   93 92   4 3 2 1

Contents

Acknowledgments

My special thanks to several people who have helped this book into the bookstores and readers' hands. At the head of the list is Tova Fliegel, Acquisitions Editor at M&T Books, whose soft voice and unflappable firmness kept my eye on the deadlines and my hands on the keyboard. Thanks also to Steve Tolman, who provided the technical review, Linda Swain for copy editing, and Stacey Evans, who designed the book and did the layouts.

Thanks to Novell, Inc. for providing a tall stack of documentation, and my gratitude to Robert Sikkema of Prime Computer, who came to my rescue with several crates of manuals.

Why This Book Is for You

Backbone network. Hot Fix. Maximum Rights Mask. Engine. Time division multiplexing. Fire phasers.

Welcome to the world of NetWare network computing! Have you already plunged in? Or been pushed into it unceremoniously? Just testing the water? In any case, you've probably heard or seen some of the NetWare commands and general networking terms. You'll meet others as you use a networked computer, join a workgroup, or decide it's time for your office to upgrade from "sneaker net" to a real NetWare network.

Where do all the terms come from? NetWare network users regularly encounter terms from hardware, software, services, protocols, standards, data security, and data management, as well as NetWare commands and terms.

What do the NetWare commands and network-related terms mean? *The NetWare Decoder* will define them for you in clear, succinct English (no jargon!), put them in context, illustrate many of them, and provide cross-references.

The dictionary format—in alphabetical order—makes it easy to look up a term and quickly go on with your network use. Whether you're a manager, student, network administrator, teacher, secretary, technical person, or newcomer to communications, The *NetWare Decoder* will be your indispensable computer-side reference.

How This Book Is Organized

Entries are listed alphabetically and appear in bold type. Words associated with the keyword also appear in bold, and related words that appear as separate entries are cross referenced in italics. Many entries are accompanied by illustrations. Occasionally, page layout has prevented an illustration from appearing immediately next to its entry, however, all illustrations are referenced at the end of the entry and the illustrations' captions clearly identify the corresponding entry.

Five appendices follow the alphabetical listings. Appendix A offers a listing of relevant terms identified with numbers or symbols; Appendix B is a table of the ASCII character set; Appendix C is a listing of NetWare commands and utilities by function; Appendix D explores ISO/OSI-compatible standards and protocols; and Appendix E provides sources of additional help.

NETWARE DECODER

AARP and AARP2 NetWare for Macintosh VAPs (v2.2) or NLMs (v3.11) containing AppleTalk Phase 1 and Phase 2 address resolution protocols. When installed on NetWare file servers, they provide connection to Macintosh computers.

abend See *abnormal end*.

abnormal end NetWare (v2.2, v3.11) operating system message *abnormal end*, indicating that the file server has been stopped because of a software or hardware problem or failure. The message then displays the recommended action: copying the server's memory contents on diskette and then turning the server's power off and restarting. Possible causes include insufficient memory, recent addition of incompatible software, setup changes, and faulty hardware.

access User entry granted into a computer network or file. The right or privilege of access may be unlimited, or it may be limited to specified files or to uses such as reading or writing. Control over access is a cornerstone of network security, intended to prevent unauthorized access to the network or to its data.

access, concurrent Access characteristic that allows several users into a network or system at the same time.

Access Control The granting or withholding of a user's rights to access a network or system for security purposes. The network supervisor is usually responsible for granting or withholding this right. If control is **mandatory**, a user's access privileges cannot be changed. Discretionary control permits changes in a user's level or degree of access. The *Access Control list* (see also *bindery*) and *capability list* (see also *user account*) are two methods of controlling users' access to a network.

Access Control is a NetWare security right that lets a user change

trustee (user) rights and also the rights granted to a directory in its Maximum Rights Mask (v2.x) or Inherited Rights Mask (v3.x, Portable NetWare). In version 2.15, this right is called Parental.

Access Control is the highest (v2.x) or second highest (v3.11) level of NetWare rights. A user granted access control can grant other users or directories Read, Write, Create, Erase, Modify, File Scan, and Access Control rights. However, NetWare v3.11 users granted Access Control cannot grant the highest level of rights—supervisory—unless they also have supervisory rights.

User (trustee) rights are assigned with the GRANT command. Rights to a directory in the Maximum Rights Masks and Inherited Rights Mask are assigned with FILER or ALLOW.

Access Control List (ACL) Access security method in which a potential user can gain entry to a network or file only by being on a list of authorized users and their access rights. The list must be searched for the user's name, which may slow the entry process.

See *bindery*.

access mode See *access right*.

access permission A user's degree or level of access to a network or system. Access is granted by the network supervisor.

access privilege See *access right*.

access privileges Term used to describe access rights in NetWare for Macintosh. A user's rights (privileges) are displayed as icons. A black tab on a folder icon on the Desktop means that security rights can be set for it. A gray folder icon means that the user has no right to open it. A gray drop box folder (with a black down arrow) can be copied but not opened (v2.x only). A gray folder with a black tab shows that the user can change the folder's security level but cannot open it.

AppleShare can display two privilege icons below the title bar: Can't Make Changes, which forbids the user from editing, deleting, and renaming files, and Can't See Documents, which prevents the user from opening a folder's files.

access right Entry privilege or degree of access granted to an individual network user, such as the rights to open, read, write to, and changing specific files. Also called access mode. For security purposes, a user is ordinarily granted the fewest rights required to perform the job.

access rights, NetWare See *Access Control.*

access, unauthorized Entry into a network, node, or data without being granted access by the security supervisor.

account balance In NetWare, the cost and payment status of a network user. Typically, a dollar amount is credited to a network user's account. Connection time, logins, disk space, and other network charges are deducted, leaving the unspent balance.

   The network supervisor (or designated account manager) controls account balances using the Account Balance option in the SYSCON User Information menu.

accounting In networking, a method of allocating space, time, and costs to users.

   In NetWare, user accounts are created for these purposes by the network supervisor using the SYSCON Supervisor Option. The account keeps track of connection time, logins, and network use; calculates and applies the charges; and, if necessary, withdraws charge privileges. The network supervisor can also add security provisions, change passwords, and designate an account manager.

accounting servers list In NetWare, a list of file servers that can charge users for their services. To view or modify the list, a supervisor or account manager enters SYSCON, selects the Accounting, the Available Topics menus, and then Accounting Servers. Pressing insert displays a list of servers that can be added to the list. The names of other servers can be viewed by pressing <Enter>. Pressing <Escape> returns you to the Accounting menu.

account manager In NetWare, a user designated by the supervisor to manage

user accounts. The account manager's responsibilities may include allocating time and restricting user access to files.

account restrictions In NetWare, limits on a user's network access to disk space and connect time. Such limits are set or changed by the supervisor or designated account manager using the Account Restrictions option in SYSCON's User Information menu.

account, user See *user account.*

acknowledge (ACK) In data communications, a positive system reply or acknowledgment of a signal or data from a sender. The ASCII reply is the control character ACK (6 hexadecimal or decimal).

ACL See *access control list.*

ACONSOLE NetWare v3.11 Asynchronous remote CONSOLE utility for remote management of file servers by supervisors and remote console operators. ACONSOLE has these functions: transferring information between a remote station and a file server; and

allowing use of a standalone computer as a remote console for asynchronous communication with a file server via modem. The standalone computer requires a directory containing the files A C O N S O L E . E X E , ACONSOLE.HLP, IBM$RUN.OVL, $RUN.OVL, LAN$RUN.OVL, SYS$ERR.DAT, SYS$HELP.DAT, and SYS$MSG.DAT. The file server must contain the loadable modules REMOTE and RS232.

acoustic coupler See *modem.*

active hub See *hub.*

activity indicator NetWare for Macintosh icon indicating a Macintosh - file server session consisting of blinking arrows displayed to the left of the Apple menu icon.

adapter A piece of hardware that allows connection of two dissimilar or noncomplementary pieces, such as two pieces of cut cable, wire and plug, or two male-male or female-female connectors.

Also a synonym for network

board. For instance, two adapter boards for the IBM PC broadband network are available for standard bus architecture and one board is available for Microchannel architecture.

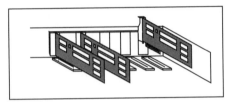

Installing a LAN adapter is just like installing any other board.

adapter request block (ARB) NetWare (v3.11) network board (adapter) command used to establish connection with a LAN driver on a file server. If the driver receives an ARB that it does not recognize, it returns this message:

```
unknown ARB request
```

ADD NAME SPACE NetWare v3.x internal command that allows multiple platforms to share files more easily. Using this command, the supervisor adds the specified name space (Mac, OS/2, NFS, FTAM) to the specified volume so that file names may be read in another operating system. DOS and OS/2 name spaces are automatically provided by NetWare. However, any other file type, such as Macintosh, must have a name space loaded before it can be copied to the file server. Once the module is loaded, you must use the ADD NAME SPACE command to enable other file types to be stored.

VREPAIR may be used to remove a name space but defaults to maintaining existing name spaces.

address The identifier of a network terminal or other node, a port, or a memory location. In networks, an address is also called **node name**.

address, base I/O Jumper or switch setting on a network board that specifies the address of an input/output port.

address, base memory Data storage buffer specified by jumper or switch settings on some network boards, such as those used for ARCnet.

address, physical A device's actual memory address. For example, a hard disk's physical address is determined by its jumper settings.

The physical address is one of three identifiers of a NetWare device; the other two are its device code and logical number.

advanced program-to-program communications (APPC) Protocol used during data transmission by IBM Systems Network Architecture for distributed mainframe computer systems using Logical Unit (LU) 6.2. It has been adapted for IBM-PC token ring networks as APPC/PC, using the LU6.2 protocol.

AFP See *AppleTalk.*

agent An operator, a person, or program that performs operations, sometimes for another entity. For example, a system component that facilitates running of an application client-server architecture is an agent.

alias An abbreviation or alternate name for a file, printer, or other device. Used as a convenience in making temporary changes in definition, program documentation, and moving among devices, systems, and applications.

ALAP protocol Communications protocol used in NetWare for the Macintosh.

alloc memory In NetWare v3.11, an expandable section of memory not required for DOS or the NetWare operating system, used to store network status information such as drive mappings, loadable module tables, and locked files, as well as current operations, including user connections, queue manager tables, service request buffers, and messages to be broadcast on the network.

all or nothing See *rollback.*

ALLOW NetWare command-line utility (v3.11, Portable NetWare) that allows a user to access an Inherited Rights Mask (directory or file rights). All users can view a mask; however, only a user granted the right of access control can add or block all, some, or none of its rights. Changes to a directory's Inherited Rights Mask do not cascade to subdirectories.

analog Characteristic of a continuously variable range of values, as in signals

or data. Analog devices include TV cameras and oscilloscopes. Analog data is transmitted by modulated signals.

analyzer, LAN See *protocol analyzer.*

analyzer, protocol See *protocol analyzer.*

API See *applications programming interface.*

AppleShare Apple Inc.'s file server and print server software for use with Macintosh client/server networks.

AppleTalk Protocols for a network of Macintosh computers (Apple, Inc.). AppleTalk is based on the ISO/OSI Reference Model and incorporates the SPX protocol. AppleTalk networks may be configured in Ethernet and token ring topologies, and use various kinds of cables. The AppleTalk Filing Protocol (AFP), for client-server architecture, runs on VAX (Digital Equipment Corp.) and other non-Macintosh servers.

AppleTalk and AFP are compatible with NetWare and are available as VAPs (v2.2) and NLMs (v3.11) in NetWare for Macintosh. Installed on NetWare servers, these VAPs and NLMs include ATALK and ATALK2 (AppleTalk Phase 1 and Phase 2), AARP and AARP2 (Phase 1 and Phase 2 address resolution protocols), AFPSPG (file services), AQS (queue services), and APS (print server services).

LAN drivers are available for several brands of Macintosh cards installed in Apple networks using Ethernet, ARCnet, token ring, and LocalTalk (Apple) networks.

application layer Layer 7 of the ISO/OSI Reference Model for open system networking. This layer governs the interface between application and network and performs file transfers and distributed database activities. (See illustration on following page.)

OSI Model
Layers

Application
Presentation
Session
Transport
Network
Data Link
Physical

The application layer of the OSI model performs file transfers and distributed database activities.

applications programming interface (API) Software for creating operating system and applications interfaces on local area networks and other distributed systems. APIs and their supporting programs are usually loaded at a workstation to provide access to servers.

APSVAP and **APSNLM** NetWare for Macintosh VAP (v2.2) or NLM (v3.11) containing print server services. When installed on NetWare file servers they provide connection to Macintosh computers.

ARB See *adapter request block.*

architecture daemon The program **npsd** that starts several Portable NetWare configuration options on the host file server. A daemon is a program that runs automatically as needed. **npsd** is activated when various tokens in the NPSConfig file are set ACTIVE. The program starts SPX with the ACTIVE token *spx*, NetWare Virtual Terminal with the token *nvt*, the IBM NetBIOS with *netbios,* and the Service Advertising Protocol with *sap.*

archive Long-term or permanent storage of seldom-used data, or the place where such storage occurs. An example is the transfer of data from a hard disk to a floppy diskette.

archive needed DOS file attribute that provides network security by automatically identifying with the designation A the files that have not been backed up after modification. The archive needed attribute is the same as MS-DOS's Archive setting function indicated by the command Attrib +a at the workstation.

File status can be viewed in the FILER menu utility (select Directory contents, the file name, and View/Set

File Information) or FLAG. A file can be backed up with the NBACKUP menu utility (select Backup Options from the main menu; then select Modified Files Only and specify Yes).

ARCnet Attached Resources Computing network (Datapoint Corp.); a token-passing network used for small LANs. An ARCnet transmits 508-byte packets at 2.5 Mbps over coaxial or fiber optic cable or unshielded twisted-pair wire. It uses either bus or star topology. See illustration on next page.

ASCII Code of 128 letters, numbers, punctuation marks, and control characters, each made up of 7 bits, used on small computers and their networks. The eighth bit (in the standard 8-bit byte) may be used to indicate parity (error-checking) or to extend the character set to include graphics. ASCII stands for American Standard Code for Information Interchange.

async See *asynchronous transmission*.

asynchronous transmission Data transmission occurring irregularly, such as from keyboard entry rather than at regular intervals (*synchronous transmission*). Each character or other block of data has a starting marker (start bit) and one or more ending markers (stop bits). Also called start-stop transmission.

Modem types that support asynchronous transmission include the Bell 103 standard (300 bps), 212 and 212A (1,200 and 300 bps), and the 224 standard and similar CCITT (European) standard (2,400 and 1,200 bps).

ATALK and **ATALK2** NetWare for Macintosh VAPs (v2.2) or NLMs (v3.11) containing the Macintosh protocol AppleTalk Phase 1 and Phase 2. When installed on NetWare servers, they provide connection to Macintosh computers.

ATOTAL NetWare command-line utility **Accounting services TOTAL.** Provides totals of network connection time, service requests, and blocks read, written, and stored. Data can be put in a file:

```
ATOTAL > totalfile
```

It can then be printed:

```
NPTINT totalfile
```

The file can also be viewed.

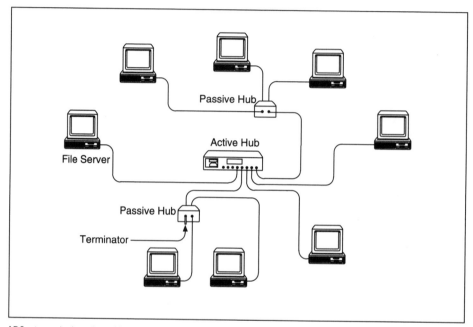

ARCnet may be based on either a star (top) or bus (below) topology.

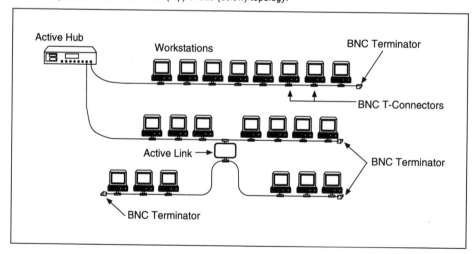

ATTACH NetWare command-line utility (v2.2, v3.11, Portable NetWare) that allows a user already logged on to a file server to log on to one or more additional servers.

The MAP command or SESSION menu utility can be used to map a network drive to the newly accessed server.

ATTACH and MAP can also be entered as a login script command.

attaching device Term used by IBM as a synonym for station.

attribute A characteristic that describes or distinguishes a piece of hardware or software, such as security attributes or database field character types.

attribute security NetWare directory and file characteristics similar to user rights, but attribute security takes precedence over user rights in protecting data.

NetWare v2.2 uses the file attributes: Archive needed, Execute Only, Hidden (file is not listed in a directory scan), Indexed, Read Audit, Read Only/Read Write, Shareable, System, Transactional, and Write Audit. NetWare v2.2's directory attributes are: Hidden, Normal, Private, and System.

NetWare v3.11 uses these file attributes: Archive needed, Copy Inhibit, Delete Inhibit, Execute Only, Hidden, Purge, Read Audit, Read Only/Read Write, Rename Inhibit, Shareable, System, Transactional, and Write Audit. NetWare v3.11 uses these directory attributes: Delete Inhibit, Hidden, Purge, Rename Inhibit, and System.

Portable NetWare file attributes are: Archive needed, Copy Inhibit, Delete Inhibit, Execute Only, Hidden, Purge, Read Only/Read Write, Rename Inhibit, Shareable, and System. Portable NetWare uses the directory attributes: Delete Inhibit, Hidden, Purge, Rename Inhibit, and System.

The status of a file's security attributes can be viewed by using the FILER menu utility: Select Directory contents, the file name, and View/Set File Information. Directory status can be viewed with FILER's Current Directory Information and Directory Attributes options or with FLAGDIR.

AUDIT NetWare Lite command for adding an 80-character (maximum) entry to an audit log when a batch file is executed. For example, to track the times a spreadsheet is accessed through a batch file, place the command

```
audit "spreadsheet accessed"
```

in the batch file. Each time it is executed, the text within quotes is added to the log. AUDIT commands can be added at the beginning and end of a batch file to indicate the duration of use. AUDIT can also be used from the command line.

audit log An audit trail in NetWare Lite, showing the date and user associated with file backup, logins, or other network operations. An audit may be generated at each server (select Audit Log from the Supervise the Network menu; then choose Audit log; and answer On to the "Turn on or off" prompt.

The option "Display audit log" consolidates the individual server logs. A log may be saved in an ASCII file with the "Save audit log to a file" option.

An audit log may be disabled by selecting Supervise the Network, Au-

dit log, Turn on or off, and Off.

audit trail Documented continuous history or log of an operation, showing its origin, transactions, supplemental data, users, and reports. An audit trail can be used, for example, in data processing, accounting, security, and network administration.

In NetWare Lite, the audit trail is called an audit log. In other versions, an audit trail can be set up with a Btrieve transaction log.

authenticate To validate or verify the integrity of transmitted data. Often done by means of a checksum digit or public key encryption.

Also to validate or verify the identity and access rights of a potential user of a network. Performed through passwords, codes, responses to questions, or other methods.

authorization Determination through a screening process that a potential user has been granted access rights to a system. Screening can be performed, for example, with an Access Control list or a capability list.

AUTOCFG NetWare for Macintosh installation VAP (v2.2) or NLM (v3.11) that configures the system and automatically loads other NetWare for Macintosh modules.

auto-endcap Printing option in CAPTURE that automatically prints or saves data when a user closes or opens an application. Though auto-endcap is a feature of the command-line utility ENDCAP, auto-endcap does not end the capture of a printer port, another ENDCAP feature.

AUTOEXEC.BAT Procedure or batch file used for startup in MS-DOS.

AUTOEXEC.NCF and **AUTOEXEC.SYS** NetWare batch file for v3.11 (NCF) or v2.2 (SYS); loaded into the file server after the operating system, initiating file execution for startup. The network supervisor uses SYSCON to create or modify the AUTOEXEC file so that it automatically executes printing services and other console commands. Select Supervisor Options and Edit System AUTOEXEC File from SYSCON's Available Topics menu. Then enter the desired commands.

AUTOEXEC can also be created or modified with a text editor.

automatic rollback See *rollback*.

backbone A network that connects other networks, allowing them to function as a single logical network. An example is NSFNET (U.S. National Science Foundation Network), a wide area network working mainly over MCI fiber-optic circuits and using TCP/IP and other protocols. Networks connect to NSFNET with T1 and T3 links. Internet (formerly ARPANET) is a worldwide backbone for wide area networks (including NSFNET) and local area networks using TCP/IP.

backing out See *rollback*.

back up To make a copy of the original on a different medium.

backup A copy of a file on a medium different from the original. For instance, a file on a hard disk can be saved to a floppy disk or to tape.

In NetWare, files can be backed up with the menu utility NBACKUP (v2.2, v3.11). The utility BACKUP.VAP (v2.2) can be used for streaming tape backup. Other NetWare-compatible backup applications may also be used.

SBACKUP.NLM (v3.11) is a server module for file backup on the Wangtek storage device (Wangtek, Inc.) attached to a host file server. SBACKUP works on the host server in conjunction with the SIDR.NLM data requester and the WANGTEK.NLM storage device driver. Servers being backed up require the modules TSA.NLM and TSA-311.NLM, which communicate with the host server via SIDR.

In Portable NetWare, backup is performed through the SCONSOLE Backup/Restore Menu.

BACKUP.VAP NetWare v2.2 loadable utility for file backup on a streaming tape drive.

backward channel See *reverse channel*.

17

BB B B

bad block See *block*.

bandwidth The range of frequencies permitting acceptable data transmission over a cable or network, usually a response 3 decibels below the reference value or one-half of it. Often used to describe the maximum operating rate.

banner Identifying information about a print job that appears on a cover sheet. Also similar information displayed on a station screen.

There are several ways to include a banner with a NetWare print job. Using the command-line utility NPRINT or CAPTURE (v2.2, v3.11), select option B. In Portable NetWare, use the option B= and enter the banner's name or text. The NetWare Lite Capture command uses this command:

```
setting b=y
```

In NetWare v2.2 or v3.11, select Print Job Configurations from the PRINTCON Available Options menu. In Portable NetWare, select Edit Print Job Configurations from the Available Options Menu. Set the Print banner field to Yes. Enter the banner's name

or text in the Name field.

baseband network Communications network of eight stations on a 200 to 300 foot coaxial cable or twisted-pair wire. Extenders allow additional stations on longer cabling. The IBM PC Baseband Network is an example.

baseband transmission Low-frequency single signal or time division multiplexed transmission of digital data for a distance of a few miles. Either coaxial cable (such as thin-Ethernet) or twisted-pair wire (such as twisted-pair Ethernet) is used.

base I/O address See address, base I/O.

base memory address See *address, base memory*.

batch file A procedure file in MS-DOS that submits commands to the operating system. An example is AUTOEXEC.BAT. NetWare batch files include AUTOEXEC.SYS (v2.2) and AUTOEXEC.NCF (v3.11).

baud A measurement of data transmission

speed used in rating networks and modems, usually defined as 1 bps (bit per second), including both data and nondata bits, such as parity (error checking) and synchronization. A network's baud is realistically measured by the baud of its slowest device. Common modem speeds are 300, 1200, 2400, 4800, and 9600 baud. Baud can roughly be converted into character speed by dividing by 10 or 11, assuming 8 data bits plus 2 or 3 start and stop bits.

baud rate See *baud*.

BCONSOLE NetWare Btrieve utility (VAP for v2.2, NLM for v3.11) that keeps track of a file server's or station's active Btrieve files; resources (files, handles, locks, and transations) in use; current users; and status, including current and total server, workstation, and network (SPX) requests processed, packets sent to and received from workstations, available and maximum request buffers and SPX packet buffers, the number of unprocessed packet buffers, and the current, maximum available, and peak num-

ber of SPX sessions. The workstation version of Btrieve also lets the user change file servers.

Bell 103 A standard in the United States for 300 bps (bits per second) modems, originated by AT&T. Provides full- or half-duplex asynchronous transmission.

Bell 212 and **212A** A standard in the United States for 300 and 1,200 bps (bits per second) modems, originated by AT&T. Provides full- or half-duplex asynchronous or synchronous transmission. 212 and 212A use different frequencies, but most 212A modems can also use 212 frequencies.

binary Number system with base 2, using only ones and zeros: One is represented by 01, two by 10, and eight by 1000. Computers have two-state or binary electronic signals that can be described as ones and zeros or true and false. Because binary digits can be long and confusing, they are often grouped in threes and handled as octal (base 8) numbers or in fours and handled as hexadecimal (base 16) numbers.

In Unix terminology, a *binary* is an executable file containing some machine language routines. A *binary file* contains data but not text, and does not utilize ASCII characters.

In the Portable NetWare configuration file NWConfig, the *binaries* token specifies the name of the network administrator's home directory, where binaries are located. This allows SCONSOLE to find them when it starts NetWare.

binary synchronous communications (BSC or **bisync)** Continuous data transmission whose constant speed is timed by signals from the sending and receiving devices. BSC is the method used within computers. Data consists of blocks of ASCII or EBCDIC (for IBM mainframes) characters. Each block begins with timing bits (synchronization, or in ASCII abbreviation, SYN), a heading notification bit (SOH), the header, which contains route information, and a text notification bit (STX). The text is followed by an end-of-text bit and a verification check bit.

bind Computer programming term meaning to translate a program's expressions into forms the machine running it can interpret and execute immediately. This can be done, for example, before execution by a compiler or by a linker (a pointer to a memory address), or at run time.

In network communication, the linking of an object name with a particular network address.

Also a session request in IBM Systems Network Architecture (SNA).

In NetWare (v3.11), a linking between an installed network board's communications protocol and its software LAN driver. The console command is BIND. In all versions of NetWare, the heading BIND in the station configuration file NET.CFG performs the same function.

Removing the link is called unbinding.

BIND NetWare v3.11 console command that links an installed network board's communication protocol to its LAN driver loaded in the file server. Used to bind one or several protocols to a

board or a protocol to one or several boards. For example, after the command BIND enter the protocol name and either the name of the LAN driver or its assigned board name. In Portable NetWare, BIND is a heading in the NET.CFG workstation configuration file.

Follow BIND with any needed protocol or driver parameters. Protocol parameters are the cabling system's network number or unique hexadecimal address and other parameters specified by the protocol. Driver parameters include DMA channel number, the frame type, interrupt number, the board's memory address, the board's I/O port number, and, for microchannel and EISA computers, the number of the slot the board occupies. These numbers should be the same as the number specified when the driver was loaded.

Note that some products are automatically bound when installed, making the BIND console command unnecessary.

A protocol-driver link can be removed with the UNBIND command.

bindery NetWare database containing information about a network that the supervisor can use to maximize security and efficient operation. The bindery contains the names of all users, devices, and other physical and logical (design) entities or objects; the properties of each object, such as user addresses, passwords, and accounts; and the data sets or values of each property.

The NetWare v2.2 bindery is contained in two hidden system files. Objects and properties are in NET$BIND.SYS and data sets are in NET$VAL.SYS. The bindery in NetWare v3.11 and Portable NetWare has three files: NET$OBJ.SYS for objects, NET$PROP.SYS for properties, and NET$VAL.SYS for data sets.

The bindery is loaded into the file server and checked each time the server is started. On a dedicated a server, the bindery is guarded by the Transaction Tracking System (TTS). On other servers, the bindery is vulnerable to system failures. Some unauthorized system changes (corruption) can be corrected with the

BINDFIX command, which builds new versions of the bindery SYS files and turns the previous files into backups with a .OLD extension.

If BINDFIX is unsuccessful, the old backup files can be restored using the BINDREST command.

BINDFIX NetWare BINDery FIX command-line utility in the SYS:SYSTEM directory that the network supervisor can use to restore bindery data that has been corrupted. These include a user's name, password, and rights, as well as error messages relating to the bindery and print spooling. BINDFIX closes the existing object, property, and data set files, then rebuilds them. It saves the previous files as backups.

In Portable NetWare, BINDFIX is also available as a maintenance utility. Access the System Administration, then select Package Management Menu, the Portable NetWare Management Menu, the Portable NetWare Maintenance Utilities Menu, and the Bindery Utilities Menu. In addition, BINDFIX can be selected through SCONSOLE by selecting the Utilities Menu and then the Services Utilities Menu.

BINDREST BINDery RESTore; a NetWare command-line utility that the network supervisor can use to restore backup bindery files (stored with the extension .OLD in the SYS:SYSTEM directory) to current (.SYS) files. BINDREST is used when the BINDFIX utility is unable to rebuild files that have been tampered with.

BIOS A computer operating system's Basic Input/Output System, low-level routines or utilities in ROM (read only memory) that control signals flowing among the controller, keyboards, disks, printers, and other devices. An example is IBM's copyrighted BIOS for its brand name personal computers.

bisync See *binary synchronous communications*.

bit The basic operating unit of conventional computers, a **bi**nary digi**t** having two possible electrical states.

BB B B

These are usually called true-false, on-off, or 0 and 1.

bit rate A measure of transmission speed, composed of the number of data bits transmitted per second, abbreviated bps.

black tab In NetWare for Macintosh, a security icon on the Desktop. A folder icon bearing a black tab indicates that the user does not have the right to open it.

See also *access privileges*.

block A unit of data; for instance, the amount of data stored in a disk sector or tape segment. The default size of one NetWare block is 4,096 bytes (4KB).

In communications, the amount of data that can be transmitted as a unit. The length of a communications block is usually variable.

A bad block is a disk area that cannot maintain data reliably. The NetWare v2.2 COMPSURF command lists bad blocks on file server disks and reformats disks. (Note that reformatting hard disks wipes out old data! See COMPSURF.) The v3.11 INSTALL loadable module can perform destructive or nondestructive tests on disk surfaces. VREPAIR (v2.2, v3.11) can fix errors in a specified volume's directories and File Allocation Tables resulting from defective disks and power outages.

The NetWare v2.2 and v3.11 SYSCON menu utility allows the network supervisor to establish accounting charges for network use based on the blocks read.

BNC connectors and **terminators** Standard type of hardware used with thin-Ethernet cabling. The hardware secures with a "bayonet" half-turn. BNC stands for either British National Connetor or Bayonet Neill Concelman. (See illustration on following page.)

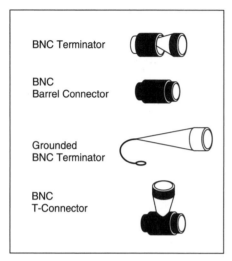

BNC components of a thin-cable Ethernet network.

board Shortened form of the term *circuit board*, the electronic circuitry for computers and peripherals, such as printers and modems. Some boards are designed to connect computers to specific types of networks, such as Ethernet and ARCnet. Such boards can be installed in stations in addition to their own circuit boards.

Boolean variable See *flag*.

boot To start up a computer system. Usually performed by a small program within the operating system known as a bootstrap loader.

DOS versions of NetWare are booted with the command SERVER, which runs the SERVER.EXE file, which in turn executes STARTUP and loads the volume (main directory). STARTUP then executes the AUTOEXEC.SYS (v2.2) or AUTOEXEC.NCF (v3.11) file, which automatically executes printing services and other console commands.

NetWare Lite is booted from the \NWLITE directory with the STARTNET command, which runs the STARTNET.BAT file. The STARTNET.BAT file loads LSL.COM and IPXODI.COM communication utilities, board drivers, and program files.

For any DOS workstation, the AUTOEXEC.BAT file loads the NetWare shell file (NET3.COM for DOS 3.x, or NET4.COM for DOS 4.x) and the IPX.COM protocol file. Shell files for expanded memory (EMSNETx.EXE), extended memory (XMSNETx.EXE), and two NetBIOS emulator programs,

NETBIOS.EXE and INT2F.COM, can also be loaded.

boot, remote See *remote boot.*

BOOTCONF.SYS NetWare file created in the process of allowing a remote boot (starting a workstation from image files on a file server). BOOTCONF.SYS contains the name given to each station's boot image file.

bps See *bit rate.*

break An interruption or stop in program execution or data transmission; a loss of communication between sender and receiver. Also a keyboard key that enables such an interruption.

BREAK NetWare login script command that lets a user interrupt script execution from the keyboard by pressing <Ctrl> C or <Ctrl><Break>. Execution requires a BREAK ON entry in the script.

BREAK OFF prevents such keyboard interruption.

BREQUEST NetWare Btrieve requestor loaded in stations, enabling resident

applications to communicate, via BSPXCOM, with the file server version of Btrieve. Versions are available for MS-DOS, OS/2, and Windows.

bridge A hardware connection between two similar networks, such as two Ethernet local area networks. A bridge makes the two networks a single logical network, accessible by any of the nodes. A *local bridge* has both input and output ports on a single device. On a *remote bridge*, input and output ports are separate but linked by a wire or cable segment.

An *internal bridge* is installed in a file server. An *external bridge* is in another computer. An external bridge may be in a *dedicated* computer, which serves only as a bridge, or it may be in a *nondedicated* computer also used as a workstation.

The term *bridge* is sometimes used interchangeably with *router*, although the two perform separate functions. However, some devices combine bridging with routing functions, such as compressing data and specifying a message path, to improve the efficiency of complex internetworks. NetWare bridges are of

this type. For instance, a NetWare bridge can route packets between Ethernet and ARCnet networks.

broadband network Communications network using broadband transmission and consisting of eight stations on a 200-foot coaxial or fiber optic cable. Expanders and distance kits permit additional stations in multiples of eight and longer cabling. The distance desired determines the type of coaxial cable used. For example, the IBM PC Broadband Network runs on coaxial cable.

broadband transmission Transmission of modulated digital or analog data, or both, at high frequency over long distances. Coaxial or fiber optic cable is used, and the signal can be single or multiplexed, that is divided into several lower frequencies, with a different signal on each. Single signals are faster than multiplexed signals.

broadcast Transmission of data to all network nodes, although the message may be addressed to a specific node.

BROADCAST NetWare v2.2 and v3.11 console command that transmits a message to all network nodes or to a list of nodes. To use the command, type BROADCAST and enter the message. If the message is going to designated stations, enclose it in quotation marks and follow it with the station numbers or (for v3.11) the user name. Separate a series of names or numbers with ther a comma, a space, or the word *and*.

A workstation can receive broadcast messages if the CASTON command-line utility has been executed. Broadcasts can be blocked with CASTOFF A (for all), but will be displayed once CASTON is executed.

Clear a broadcast message by pressing <Ctrl><Enter>.

broadcasting, single route See *ROUTE*.

broadcasting, all routes See *ROUTE*.

BROLLFWD NetWare Btrieve workstation utility used to maintain data integrity when current data is lost because of system failure. BROLLFWD reconstructs the data by

BB**B**B

updating a backup version from a transaction log from the time of backup to the time of system failure.

Logging for any file must be specified during Btrieve configuration and expressed in a BLOG.CFG file in a BLOG directory for each volume.

BROUTER NetWare Btrieve file server application that enables SPX communication (via BSPXCOM) between Btrieve and applications on other servers. Available as a VAP for NetWare v2.2 and an NLM for NetWare v3.11.

BRQPARMS In NetWare Btrieve, an OS/2 variable for defining Btrieve Requestor options for an application.

BSC See *binary synchronous communications.*

BSETUP NetWare Btrieve program loaded on the server and used to configure or reconfigure Btrieve, setting the options for number of files open, handles, record locks, transactions,

and files opened per transaction; record and page size; number of sessions; and file logging.

BSPXCOM NetWare Btrieve program that uses the SPX protocol for transmission of Btrieve files from other servers.

Btrieve NetWare Record Management System, a VAP for NetWare v2.2 and an NLM for NetWare v3.11. A database management system used to assist in network administration, programming, and development. Two Btrieve versions are available—one for a station installation, where all processing is performed on files retrieved by operating system calls, and one for a file server, available from a requestor program installed on the workstations. Applications are interchangeable between the two Btrieve versions.

Features include files up to 4 GB in size, an unimited number of records, 14 data types, and key indexing with a maximum of 24 indexes per file. Data integrity and

security measures include data encryption, file ownership, file and record locks, logging of transactions, and updating of backup files from the transaction log (roll forward) in case of current data loss.

The server version consists of the BTRIEVE record manager and the BSPXCOM station communications program. BREQUEST requestor programs are available for MS-DOS, OS/2, and Windows. BROUTER allows Btrieve access from other file servers.

BTRIEVE NetWare Btrieve program (VAP for v2.2 and NLM for v3.11) that handles record management, including disk input/output, record and file locks, and logging of file change requests.

buffer An area of computer memory set aside for temporary data storage.

buffer/driver See *driver*.

bulletin board In general, a computer network system (abbreviated BBS) that allows users to write files to be read by all other users. The BBS is intended to be an information exchange.

NetWare for Macintosh provides for a bulletin board folder to which all trustees (users with folder rights) are granted the rights Read and File Scan. These trustee rights are themselves referred to as a Bulletin Board. Trustees who wish to write to a bulletin board folder must have been granted the rights *Write to files* and *Create files/folders*.

bus A communications path or channel that connects computer devices, either internally or externally. For example, an internal bus connects processors and controllers. An external bus may connect a computer and printers or other peripherals. Bus also describes a straight cable that connects nodes in a bus network.

bus driver See *driver*.

bus network A network whose logical topology is in a straight line, with all nodes connected to a central, or trunk, cable called a bus or a network bus.

Ethernet uses a bus topology.

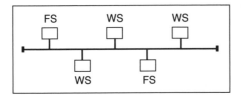

The bus network topology uses one central cable.

bus, network See *bus network*.

byte A group of data bits that functions as a unit. The standard byte has eight bits, although this is not always the case. ASCII, for example, uses 7-bit bytes.

NETWARE DECODER

C High-level language that is regarded as close to assembly language. It provides direct access to basic machine facilities. Used for operating systems, communications packages, input/output drivers and file control, and other low-level functions for applications.

Libraries of C routines can be called in NetWare. In v3.11, they are available as applications programming interfaces (APIs).

cable Term used to describe any electrical conductor that connects network devices and transmits data. Technically cable is an insulated conductor or group of conductors with a common insulator.

Coaxial cable consists of two concentric conductors. The inner conductor, an insulated wire, carries the signal. The outer conductor, solid or mesh metal, is the ground and also protects against signal interference. This conductor is covered with plastic.

The definition also includes wire whose cover is a conductor, such as *twisted pair*. Twisted-pair cable is a group of twisted-pair wires, such as 4 or 25, bound by a protective covering.

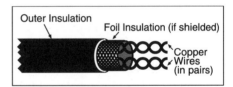

These are the standard parts of twisted-pair cable.

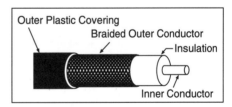

These are the standard pieces of a coaxial cable.

Ribbon cable is flat, with multiple wires side by side within a protective cover. It is often used to connect peripheral devices to internal computer cards.

A *patch cable* temporarily connects communications lines.

cable adapter See *adapter*.

cache An area of computer memory set aside for frequently used data in order to speed up operations. Some caches are general purpose. Others are for specific operations, such as NetWare's read-ahead cache on Executable and Read Only files.

NetWare v2.2 and v3.11 assigns file server cache memory for directory entries, a file read from disk, the File Allocation Table (FAT) containing each file's disk location, the FAT index known as Turbo Fat, the hash table that points to a file's cache location, and space for data and (in v3.11) NLMs. Unassigned cache memory is available for other purposes. In v2.2, cache block (or buffer) size is 4 KB. In v3.11, each block can be 4, 8, or 16 KB; the size is set with SERVER.EXE.

Portable NetWare, which runs as a process (program) on the host, uses the host's cache rather than having its own general cache. Portable NetWare does have a local or spot (read-ahead) cache, which contains the file block that comes right after the block that is being used. Cache blocks have the same size as the host's block size, set in the NWConfig file with the token *cache_block_size*.

Cache blocks are assigned by the operating system on an as- needed basis from a *buffer pool*. When an NLM or other component is removed from the system, the cache block reverts to the pool.

cache buffer pool See *cache*.

cache, file See *cache*.

call A program instruction that causes another program or routine to execute, then returns to the main program. A call from a high-level language to a routine in C or to a machine language can speed execution of the main program.

In NetWare, C routines can be called from libraries.

call-back modem See *modem, callback*.

capability In computer and data security, the definition of a user's right to use a file, device, or other object.

This is in contrast to an access right, which defines the object's availability to the user.

capability list Method of granting or denying a potential user's access to a system based on the user's listed capabilities. Considered faster than searching an access control list.

In NetWare, called the *user account*.

CAPTURE NetWare command-line utility that sends an application's print job to a network printer in cases where the application can direct the job only to a station's LPT port (for a local parallel printer). In v2.2 and v3.11, CAPTURE also can be used to send data to a file and print screen displays.

CAPTURE can be enabled automatically by including it in the station's login script.

Options allow the user to configure a print job. If a job instead is configured with the menu utility PRINTCON, the configuration can be specified in CAPTURE with the option *job*. CAPTURE can end a job automatically with the option *autoendcap*, time the next print job using *timeout*, or manually send the job to the print queue with the command-line utility ENDCAP.

In NetWare Lite, the command

```
net capture
```

captures a port. The command

```
net capture del
```

deletes a port capture.

carrier In network communications, a continuous wave at a specified frequency range that is modulated for data transmission. A sine wave is often used. Modulation of the wave's amplitude (AM), frequency (FM), or phase is possible.

carrier sense multiple access (CSMA) Network protocol permitting station transmission whenever the line is not being used. A station competes with other stations using the contention access method, in which a station senses when the line is not being used, transmits a packet, then releases the line. CSMA does not prevent collisions with other messages since the transmitting station's sig-

nal may not have reached another station before it transmits. Or two stations may transmit at the same time.

Two collision reduction variants are *collision avoidance (CA)* and the more widely used *collision detection (CD)*.

carrier sense multiple access, collision avoidance (CSMA/CA) Using the CSMA protocol, a station transmits only after it has made sure that the line is not in use, thereby avoiding collision between its signal and another already on the line. CA uses time division multiplexing to separate contending signals. Token ring is a technology that uses collision avoidance.

carrier sense multiple access, collision detection (CSMA/CD) Using the CSMA protocol, a station transmits before checking whether the line is already in use. The station retransmits after an algorithmically-determined period of time if it detects a collision between its signal and another already on the line.

CSMA/CD is codified in IEEE Standard 802.32. The protocol used by Ethernet networks is similar.

carrier system See *frequency division multiplexing*.

CASTOFF NetWare v2.2, v3.11 and Portable NetWare command-line utility that prevents network messages from reaching the station, for example, when they could disrupt an ongoing operation. Messages are displayed after the CASTON command-line utility is executed.

To block messages from stations only use CASTOFF To also block file server messages, enter `CASTOFF A[LL]`.

In NetWare Lite, a station's ability to receive messages is controlled with the Receive Messages command.

CASTON NetWare command-line utility (v2.2, v3.11, Portable NetWare) that allows a workstation to receive network messages. Clear a message from the screen by pressing <Ctrl><Enter>.

In NetWare Lite, a station's abil-

ity to receive messages is controlled with the Receive Messages command.

CCITT Comité Consultatif Internationale de Télégraphique et Téléphonique (International Consultative Committee on Telegraphy and Telephony), a member body of the International Telecommunications Union. CCITT recommends specifications for communications circuits, modems, packet switching, and other aspects of telecommunications. The recommendations are often followed in many countries, particularly in Europe, or adopted by other organizations as standards. An example is CCITT's recommendation V.22 bis for 2,400 bps modems.

CFS See *convert file system.*

channel A data transmission path, either a frequency or hardware. Also called a circuit or a transmission line. A transmission signal may be a single frequency or channel, or it can use several channels at once. The connection of a device to a DMA (direct memory access) controller chip is also called a channel.

In network security, a legitimate channel is called an overt channel. A covert channel is devised for unauthorized entry and data transfer. For example, a covert storage channel could illegitimately intercept a file in a legitimate file transfer. A covert timing channel manipulates processor timing to divert a data stream.

character A single letter, digit, or symbol used in text, text transmission, and formatting as, for example, the ASCII characters. Each character takes up a single byte.

NetWare supports one-byte characters but not non-ASCII multibyte characters, such as Chinese or Japanese idiograms.

characters per second (cps) Measurement of data transmission speed, with 10 characters per second approximating 100 baud. This is based on the requirement of 10 or 11 bits per character, including 8 data bits, 1 start bit, and 1 or 2 stop bits.

check digit A single digit added to numeri-

cal data to ensure entry and transmission accuracy and also data security. The original sum of the digits is compared with the sum after entry or transmission. An inequality indicates an error.

checksum A calculation included with a packet to verify that data has been transmitted accurately. The calculation is a sum representing the value of the data bits in a transmitted packet. The receiver again calculates the value of the data bits, and compares its sum with that of the transmitted value. Identical values mean that the data was correctly transmitted. A difference in values represents an unidentified transmission error.

When configuring a NetWare v3.11 file server to use the IP Tunnel (which connects NetWare to an IP internetwork), you can also include a User Datagram Protocol (UDP) checksum as an option of the LOAD IPTUNNEL command.

In Portable NetWare, checksum calculation is an automatic function of SCONSOLE when volumes are being backed up or restored.

child In hierarchical data structures, such as data trees, and object-oriented programming, a node or object that is descended from one above it in the hierarchy. The child inherits characteristics from its predecessor.

In Unix, a *child process* is the new process formed when an existing process replicates itself using the call fork. The original process is then known as the parent process.

In the NetWare volume hierarchy, a child is a data set that has no descendants, such as a file in a directory. In this case, the directory is a parent. For example, both terms, "child" and "parent," are used in v3.11 SBACKUP's Restore Options screen, displayed when data is being restored to a file server.

A NetWare directory inherits rights that are set in the Maximum Rights Mask (v2.2) of the directory or volume above it. Changes in a directory's mask are automatically made in a child directory, unless otherwise set.

In NetWare v3.11, the Inherited Rights Mask of a child directory does not inherit changes made to the parent directory. This rule also applies to the Inherited Rights Mask of a file.

CHKDIR A NetWare v3.11 and Portable NetWare command-line utility, CHecK DIRectory provides information about a specific directory and its volume, including maximum space, the amount of space in use, and the amount available.

To obtain more information about the volume, use the CHKVOL utility.

CHKVOL NetWare command-line utility that provides information about a volume. In v2.2, CHKVOL includes the volume name and size, space occupied by files, and free space. In the v3.11 and Portable NetWare versions, CHKVOL gives more detailed information about space use, including the amount occupied by active and deleted files.

circuit A network of closed paths consisting of an electrical conductor or conductors. A circuit is also called a transmission line or channel. A circuit of several stations is called a multipoint circuit.

circuit switching Establishing of a telephone line path between telephones or modems. The path must be acknowledged before a message can be transmitted.

classification, security See *security classification*.

clearance, security See *security clearance*.

clear console screen In NetWare v2.2, this function is performed with the OFF console command. In v3.11, either CLS or OFF is used.

CLEAR MESSAGE NetWare v2.2 console command that removes a brief message displayed after the console command MONITOR is executed to summarize workstation use.

CLEAR STATION NetWare console command (v2.2, v3.11) used when a workstation crashes, to totally sever the workstation's connection with the file server. The command closes files and breaks the workstation/file server communication link. To use, enter the command, followed by the workstation number (available through the MONITOR console command). CLEAR STATION does not break any links the station has to other file servers.

CLIB NetWare Loadable Module in v3.11; the CLIB is a library of C language routines used with several other NetWare Loadable Modules.

client In networks, a node that requests service from another node. An example is a workstation that requests access to a mainframe, a printer, or another workstation, but is not necessarily dependent on it.

Client status can be formalized in distributed data processing and in client/server network architecture, in which the client node is always dependent on a server node for some operations.

client/server architecture Communications and data management architecture in which some operations are always handled by specific hardware and software. For instance, file transfer or some large database services will always be handled by a station called a server. Other stations wanting to use these services are clients and must request access to the server. The architecture is sometimes also called requestor/server.

NetWare v2.2 and v3.11 is designed for client/server architecture, with the operating system and other network services loaded into one or more MS-DOS or OS/2 file servers, from which client workstations can request services.

NetWare Lite client workstations and servers use MS-DOS. Macintosh servers are accessible with NetWare for Macintosh. Portable NetWare client stations can request services from either a Unix host or MS-DOS, OS/2, or Macintosh file servers.

CLIENT.EXE In NetWare Lite, an executable file loaded into a workstation, allowing it to use files and services on workstations that are designated as servers (using SERVER.EXE).

CLS NetWare v3.11 CLear Screen console command. The OFF console commands also clears the console's screen.

CMOS Complementary Metal Oxide Semiconductor. A CMOS is a low-power computer chip used to store a station's or system's configuration information, including memory size and type, and number of disk drives. The CMOS memory is battery-maintained and independent of the operating system.

CMPQ$RUN.OVL NetWare overlay file containing black-and-white equivalents for color specifications in screen menus, text, and various messages. The file is used for non-IBM monochrome monitors.

coaxial cable See *cable*.

code Term used as a synonym for computer program, particularly one written in machine language (language that can be directly executed by the computer).

Coding is the adapting, sending, and receiving of transmissions according to a stated set of rules.

collision In data communications, the attempted transmission of a signal on particular path by more than one workstation at the same time.

A workstation may handle collisions with collision avoidance, in which the workstation avoids collisions by not transmitting until it has checked that the path is clear. One widely used collision avoidance protocol is CSMA/CA (Carrier Sense Multiple Access/Collison Avoidance).

A workstation can also handle collisions with collision detection, in which it transmits without checking for a clear path, then retransmits if a collision occurs. Collision detection, as in the protocol CSMA/CD (Carrier Sense Multiple Access/Collision Detection) is the more popular method.

color palette In NetWare, a color combination used for screen text, menus, and other messages and displays. A palette is specified with the COLORPAL menu utility.

COLORPAL NetWare COLOR PALette menu utility, which specifies colors for five palettes: Palette 0 (lists, menus, and normal text), Palette 1 (headers and background), Palette 2 (help screens), Palette 3 (error messages), and Palette 4 (exit and alert messages).

    In NetWare v2.2 and v3.11, colors in a directory can be modified by supervisors. In v2.2, users with Read, File Scan, Write, and Erase rights can also make modifications. In v3.11, the trustee (user) Read, Write, Create, and Erase rights are required. In Portable NetWare, any user can make changes.

    COLORPAL default palettes are set for IBM color adapters. For non-IBM monochrome monitors, change the machine type to CMPQ in the SHELL.CFG file.

COM1, COM2 Designations for the first and second serial ports on IBM and compatible computers.

COMCHECK NetWare COMmunications CHECK command-line utility, used to test file server/workstation communications. After being run, COMCHECK reports whether the shell has been loaded and whether the network board is in communication with the network; it verifies the workstation's unique name and displays the correct date and time.

command-line utilities NetWare utilities entered from the DOS prompt (v2.2, v3.11) that permit changes in rights and attributes, a user's server and station access and preferences, printing specifications, file manipulation, and display of directory and volume information.

    In Portable NetWare, command-line utilities are used by the administrator to view user information, make host-station text file conversions, maintain the bindery, upgrade the file system after installation of a new version of Portable NetWare, and control the network environment.

common carrier Communications system uniformly available to the public

and either government owned or government regulated. Telephone companies are examples.

communication buffer See *packet receive buffer*.

comparison See *conditionals*.

compression, data Reduction of the size of a data block so that it takes up less space in disk storage or less time and cost to transmit. The two main methods are differential and hierarchic compression. Differential compression is often used on predictable data, such as an alphabetical listing. In this case, the first or last letters of each entry are eliminated and replaced, for instance, by an representing the number of similar characters removed from the entry and the preceding entry.

Hierarchic compression is used for hierarchical data, such as database records. A redundant field might be eliminated, or several fields combined.

COMPSURF NetWare v2.2 DOWN command for testing and reformatting a hard disk. Note that using COMPSURF destroys all data on the hard disk! (The administrator will have to restore from a backup copy.)

With all workstation software closed and users logged out (verify with the FCONSOLE or SESSION menu utilities), enter the DOWN console command to close the operation system. Back up hard disk files before proceeding so that you may restore this data later. Then issue COMPSURF. The lengthy test and reformatting process identifies bad blocks, which are listed and can be printed on a parallel printer attached to port LPT1.

COMSPEC NetWare login script command that enters the drive letter and path of the DOS command interpreter (command processor), usually COMMAND.COM and the drive where it is located, as in the following example:

```
COMSPEC = c:COMMAND.COM
```

concentrator Communications hardware that manages transmissions by modifying signals. For example, a concentrator can handle transmissions between many low-speed asynchro-

nous channels and a smaller number of high-speed synchronous channels. It may employ time division multiplexing. Used as a hub in a star topology network, a concentrator allows the addition of more stations or cabling.

concurrency Property of a system that allows multiple operations to take place at the same time. Concurrent access, for instance, allows several users to access the same data at the same time.

conditionals In NetWare, relationships of equality and inequality used in conditional statements or rules in the IF...THEN (v2.2) and IF...THEN...ELSE (v3.11) login script commands. Netware allows the following conditionals to be identified as variables:

Conditional Statement	Symbol
is less than	<
is less than or equal to	<=
equal	IS *or* = *or* EQUALS
exact equality	==
not equal	IS NOT *or* != *or* <> *or* # or DOES NOT EQUAL or NOT EQUAL TO
is greater than or equal to	>=
is greater than	>

CONFIG NetWare console command (v2.2, v3.11) that displays configuration information about the file server or bridge/router. In v2.2, CONFIG displays the network address, server-bridge/router type and setting, and disk drive type and setting. In v3.11, CONFIG displays the file server name, internal network number, and each network board's hardware settings, protocols, cabling scheme, frame type, and name.

CONFIG.SYS MS-DOS configuration file created by some applications. CONFIG.SYS is located in the root

directory and used when booting a workstation.

The file contains, for example, the number of buffers and the number of drives. CONFIG.SYS can be modified to reflect changes in the system, such as installation of device drivers. For instance, installation of the NetWare Open Data-Link Interface (ODI) may involve use of the IBM LAN Support and DXMAID programs. DXMAID creates a CONFIG.SYS file.

configuration information The following NetWare v2.2 console commands provide information about the file server configuration: CONFIG, DISPLAY NETWORKS, DISPLAY SERVERS, NAME, SPOOL, UPS, VERSION, and VOLUMES.

NetWare v3.11 console commands are: CONFIG, DISPLAY NETWORKS, DISPLAY SERVERS, MODULES, NAME, PROTOCOL, SPEED, SPOOL, UPS STATUS, UPS TIME, VERSION, and VOLUMES.

confirmation box A NetWare v3.11 screen displayed after a user makes a significant change, such as exiting an NLM or deleting a volume. The box requires confirmation (Yes) before the command will be executed. No cancels the command.

connection number An operating system control number assigned to each workstation each time it attaches to a file server. The USERLIST command-line utility displays a list of all users of a file server. The WHOAMI command-line utility displays a workstation user's control number on each attached file server.

connectivity Ability of hardware and software to be connected to a network that accepts different hardware brands and operating systems.

For example, Macintosh computers (Apple Computer Inc.) can be connected to a network of DOS-based devices using NetWare for Macintosh.

connector A plug, jack, or other physical interface used on a network. Thin-Ethernet cable requires BNC barrel connectors; a BNC T- connector has a plug for a BNC jack on a network

board. Thick-Ethernet cable uses DIX plug and socket connectors or N- series plug and jack connectors. Twisted-pair wire uses RJ45 plugs and jacks.

console A computer terminal, especially the main terminal that a manager uses to control a system.

In NetWare, a console is a terminal either directly connected to a file server or connected via the RCONSOLE or ACONSOLE menu utilities. From the console, the network supervisor or designated console operator sends console commands to the file server and performs other server operations.

Console commands, issued only from a console, are used to monitor and control the file server and its use by stations.

CONSOLE NetWare v2.2 command-line utility that allows a nondedicated file server or external bridge to be used as a console and permits that server or bridge to execute console commands.

contention A method of network access in which a station can seize the line any time it is free and transmit over it. Contention is used by the CSMA/CA and CSMA/CD protocols and by Ethernet. This access method contrasts with other methods, such as polling and token passing, that arbitrarily restrict a station's transmission opportunities.

convert file system (CFS) Portable NetWare command-line utility used to upgrade the file system after installation of a new software version. To use, enter the command and either argument C (file system consistency check that rebuilds the file system tree) or argument U (upgrade the system):

```
cfs -C or cfs -U
```

To print the current file system version, use argument V.

copy Files may be copied from one directory to another in NetWare v2.2, v3.11, and Portable NetWare with the FILER menu utility and the NCOPY command-line utility.

Copy Inhibit NetWare v3.11 file security attribute that prevents users of Macin-

tosh workstations from copying a file, even if they have Read and File Scan rights to that file.

covert channel See *channel*.

covert storage channel See *channel*.

covert timing channel See *channel*.

CRC See *cyclic redundancy check*.

Create NetWare directory right that permits users to create subdirectories and files. To open a file after creating, writing to it, and closing it, the user must also have the Create right. Otherwise, the user creates a drop box directory and the file cannot be opened after it is created, written to, and closed.

crosstalk In data communications, a signal that inadvertently crosses over from one channel to another, creating interference.

CSMA See *carrier sense multiple access*.

CSMA/CA See *carrier sense multiple access/collision avoidance*.

CSMA/CD See *carrier sense multiple access/collision detection*.

currency indicator A pointer or position in a database. Also called a currency symbol.

currency symbol See *currency indicator*.

cyclic redundancy check (CRC) Also known as the frame check sequence, CRC is a mathematical method used to verify that data has been transmitted accurately. The data bits are calculated through several exclusive-OR gates. CRC is also called polynomial code, because it treats bit strings as representations of polynomials with coefficients of zeros and ones only. All arithmetic is done modulo 2, with no carries or borrows.

NETWARE DECODER

D2U Portable NetWare command-line utility that converts MS-DOS text files into UNIX host text files, principally by removing MS-DOS line feeds at line ends. D2U works on either a host or a UNIX station.

DC Component of the IPX/SPX protocol stack.

daemon In UNIX terminology, a program that performs an operation without receiving a user command. Some daemons operate automatically, others at specified intervals. An example is the Portable NetWare architecture daemon *npsd*, which starts the IBM NetBIOS when triggered by an active token in the NPSConfig file.

   The alternate spelling *demon* is never used in the UNIX environment.

data control language A group of commands in Structured Query Language (SQL) that provides security to relational databases. The com-mand GRANT allows access and REVOKE withholds it.

data definition language Structured Query Language (SQL) commands that permit creation of tables and indexes in relational databases.

Data Encryption Standard (DES) Widely used algorithm for encryption and decryption of sensitive data using a 56-bit key to encipher 64-bit data blocks. DES is available on special computer chips.

datagram Data transmission method that divides a message into individual packets and sends them in random order. Delivery is not guaranteed. The message is reassembled correctly after all the packets are received. This is the method used by the NetWare IPX network layer protocol. It is also used by the User Datagram Protocol (UDP), a transport layer protocol of TCP/IP, and by IP.

   A datagram serves the same func-

tion as a frame.

An alternate method is the *virtual circuit*, in which all packets are sent and received in order.

data link escape (DLE) In data communications, a signal from a receiver to a sender to terminate a transmission before it is completed. The ASCII reply is the control character DLE (10 hexidecimal, 16 decimal). This is also known as *reverse interrupt*. DLE is also used to initiate *transparent mode* transmission.

Data-Link layer Layer 2, the hardware layer, of the ISO/OSI Reference Model of data communications. Its services include formatting data packets for transmission, assuring that packets are received correctly, and determining if incoming packets are addressed to the local node.

The Data-Link layer, along with Layer 1, the Physical layer, is encompassed by Ethernet and other TCP/IP network protocols that communicate with the IP layer. The Data-Link layer receives an outgoing data packet from the IP layer, adds a data-link header, encloses the packet in a data-link frame, and transmits the packet to the receiving node. There the data link layer eliminates the packet's data-link header and turns the packet over to the IP layer.

data manipulation language Database-oriented computer language that allows users to easily query the database and add, delete, or change data. Structured Query Language (SQL) uses a data manipulation language for relational databases.

data protection See *security, data.*

data recovery See *salvage.*

data security See *security, data.*

data set A related group of data entities, such as the records in a database, the files in a subdirectory, and the subdirectories in a directory.

Also the original term for a modem.

date indicator variables In NetWare, various ways of displaying the date,

specified in a login script. Choices are day, the number of the day of the month; *day_of_week*, the name of the day of the week; month, the number of the month; *month-name*; *nday_of_week*, the number of the day of the week, beginning with Sunday; *short_year*, the year number, omitting the century, such as 93; and *year*, the full number.

DCB See *disk coprocessor board*.

DCB.DSK NetWare v3.11 NLM containing the disk driver for the disk coprocessor board (DCB). When installing NetWare, the file is loaded after running the installer file SERVER.EXE. The command to load DCB.DSK can be placed in a STARTUP.NCF file so that the driver will be for loaded automatically when the system is booted.

DCONFIG NetWare Driver CONFIGuration console command (v2.2) and command-line utility (v3.11, Portable NetWare) used to change LAN driver information in the IPX.COM shell file (all versions)

or NET$OS.EXE or ROUTER.EXE (v2.2). Information includes network address, shell node address and configuration, controller type, and number of buffers.

In v2.2, DCONFIG replaces SCONFIG used in earlier versions. DCONFIG displays the current information, which can then be changed.

In v3.11, the information should be the same as that for the station's network board. As an alterative, the WSGEN command-line utility (v3.11) or SHGEN (Portable NetWare) can be used to create a new IPX.COM file.

DDCMP (Digital Data Communication Message Protocol) Byte-count-oriented communications protocol (Digital Equipment Corp.). DDCMP uses a packet header containing information about how many data characters are in the packet and assigns a packet sequence number. Each packet also contains a cyclic redundancy check (CRC) for transmission accuracy. The destination station keeps track of which packets have been received.

DDCMP can be used for either synchronous or asynchronous transmission at either half- or full-duplex. Transmission can be serial or parallel and either point-to-point or multipoint.

decipher To decode a message, restoring it to plain language. The term *decrypt* is also used, though *decipher* is preferred internationally.

decode A synonym for *decipher*. Decoding is the process of converting a digital signal into an analog signal, particularly speech, as in transmission over a switched (telephone) line.

decrypt See *decipher*.

dedicated Description of a network device used exclusively for a single purpose; for example, a computer that is used only as a file server or a router is a dedicated file server or dedicated router.

In NetWare, a dedicated IPX driver is an IPX.COM file created with WSGEN (v2.2, v3.11) or SHGEN (Portable NetWare).

A network device that is also used for other purposes is called nondedicated. For example, a computer that is used as both a file server and a station is a nondedicated server.

dedicated server See *dedicated*.

default The current value or characteristic of a variable. Most variables have initial values that are assigned by a hardware manufacturer or software publisher and used unless redefined by a user. In NetWare, for example, the initial default palettes in the COLORPAL menu utility are set for color, but can be changed to work on monochrome.

delete Erasure of data from a computer disk or file. Many applications make deletion a two-step process, allowing the material to be restored after the first step.

Delete NetWare for Macintosh (v2.15) access right. In subsequent versions, the name is changed to Erase.

DELETED.SAV In NetWare v3.11 and Portable NetWare, a hidden directory automatically created in the SYS volume. The directory contains files that have been deleted but not purged.

Delete Inhibit A NetWare v3.11 security attribute automatically assigned to a file or directory when it is designated Read Only. Delete Inhibit prevents users who have been granted the Erase right from deleting the file or directory. However, users with the Modify right can remove Delete Inhibit and erase the file or directory.

delimiter A bit, character, blank space, or other marker that separates portions of a transmitted message or indicates the end of the message. In asynchronous transmission, start and stop bits separate characters. The ASCII null character is often used to mark the end-of-message.

demodulation Demodulation is when a modem restores a signal to digital pulses after the signal was changed from digital to sound frequencies (modulation) for transmission. De-

modulation occurs in computer-to-computer transmission over a telephone line.

More generally, the restoration to its original form of a carrier whose frequency, amplitude, or phase has been altered for data transmission.

descriptor An identifier, such as an index entry. In data security, a descriptor is similar to a capability, but provides access only to a single process.

destination Node name, network address, or user name to which a network message is transmitted.

device driver See *driver*.

DGroup memory In MS-DOS, a group is a 64K byte memory area addressed in object (machine-executable) files. The DGroup is an area defined by the DOS Linker.

In NetWare, DGroup memory is the location of the file server memory pool.

diagnostic A test that determines such information as whether a network

device is functioning correctly.

In UNIX terminology, a diagnostic is the error message displayed after a hardware or software malfunction.

dial-up line A telephone line to which a network or freestanding computer communication connection is made in order to complete a circuit with another computer or network.

differential transmission Method of data transmission of a signal at a different voltage over each of two twisted wires. At the destination, the signal is the voltage difference. Used in order to overcome line interference, which would be the same on both wires.

digital Having discrete rather than continuous (analog) values. For example, a computer uses two values. A digital signal (*digital transmission*) uses several specific values.

Digital Data Communication Message Protocol See *DDCMP*.

digital switching In switched (telephone) systems, changing voice (analog) data to digital data for transmission.

digital transmission See *digital*.

direct memory access (DMA) Direct transfer of data between a device and a computer's random access memory (RAM) without control by the central processing unit (CPU). DMA is usually accomplished with a specialized computer chip. The method may also "steal cycles" from the CPU. DMA speeds up data transfer and reduces the CPU's workload.

directory A data set in hierarchical data structures that contains other data sets. A directory may contain files, subdirectories, or both. The directory is the organizational structure of UNIX, MS-DOS, and other operating systems. In MS-DOS the main directory is called the **root directory** and subordinate directories are called directories or subdirectories. In the Macintosh operating system the main directory is the **finder**, visualized on the **desktop**. Other directories are called **folders**. The UNIX

main directory is the **home directory**.

In NetWare, the highest organizational level is the file server. Each server's main directory is called a *volume*; subdirectories are called directories. NetWare automatically creates the SYS volume and four directories: SYSTEM, for system administration; PUBLIC, for regular network use; LOGIN, containing procedures for entering the network; and MAIL, for electronic mail. User-defined volumes must be created during NetWare installation. New directories can be created at any time.

In v3.11 and Portable NetWare, a hidden directory DELETED.SAV is also created automatically for storage of deleted but not purged files.

Directories can be reached via a station's operating system or directly through NetWare. In NetWare, the user maps a path to a disk drive with the MAP command-line utility or MAP INSERT. Each entity in a directory path is demarked either by a / (slash) or by a \ (backslash) as in MS-DOS. The path may be included in a login script for future use.

Directory Mask In Portable NetWare, a right restricting access to NetWare directories to NetWare users and forbidding access by other users of the host computer.

directory rights See *rights, directory*.

DISABLE LOGIN NetWare v2.2, v3.11 console command that keeps users from logging in to the file server. For example, the network supervisor can execute this command when he or she needs to perform hardware or file maintenance. The ENABLE LOGIN console command restores use.

DISABLE TRANSACTIONS NetWare v2.2 console command for temporarily turning off the Transaction Tracking System (TTS). Its principal purpose is to permit testing of applications that might conflict with TTS.

DISABLE TTS NetWare v3.11 console command for temporarily turning off the transaction tracking system (TTS). Its principal purpose is to permit testing of applications that might conflict with TTS.

DISK NetWare v2.2 console command that allows the operating system to chart the physical status of the attached disk drives and make indicated corrections. DISK can also be used to show the drives' status for any specified volume.

disk drivers NetWare v2.2 and v3.11 routine that enables communication with a hard disk. In v2.2, disk drivers are defined in the INSTALL.EXE program and are linked in to the NetWare operating system.

In v3.11, disk driver files (extension .DSK) are loadable modules. For a new network, the driver is loaded after running the NetWare installer file SERVER.EXE using LOAD. The driver can then be placed in a STARTUP.NCF file for automatic operation each time the system is booted.

disk coprocessor board (DCB) Specialized network board that acts as an independent extension of the main host central processing unit (CPU). The coprocessor stores and retrieves disk drive data. A DCB speeds data han-

dling and also allows more efficient use of the main CPU.

NetWare v2.2 and v3.11 can support up to four DCBs, each of which can have eight controllers. Each controller can support two disk drives. DCBs work with ISA (80286) and EISA architectures.

DISKSET NetWare utility that identifies an external hard disk drive for a DCB and enables hard disk drive/ file server communication. The identifying information, which is stored in a programmable chip on the board, includes disk type, controller address or number, and channel number. Each external drive must be defined for each DCB.

Additionally, DISKSET can be used to backup or restore external drive information and to change perviously entered information. In v3.11, it can also be used to format an external drive.

IN v2.2, DISKSET is a *down command*. In v3.11, it is an NLM.

disk space restrictions Assignment of NetWare (v2.2, v3.11) disk space for

accounting purposes. Such assignment is made by the network supervisor or a designated user account manager who has file security rights.

DISMOUNT NetWare v2.2 and v3.11 console command that prevents users from accessing any volume that has been made available with the MOUNT console command. DISMOUNT allows the network supervisor to complete maintenance of the volume without closing down the file server on which it resides. Dismounting unused volumes frees cache memory for other uses.

Note: With NetWare v3.11, the SYS volume can be dismounted. However, this effectively disables the server since the Bindery is no longer accessible.

DISPLAY NetWare v2.2 login command that sends an ASCII text file to network stations and displays it when the stations' users log in.

DISPLAY NETWORKS NetWare v2.2 and v3.11 console command that displays a list of networks known to the bridge/router. Each network is identified by its network address, the number of networks that must be crossed to reach it (called *hops*), and the amount of time required to transmit a packet in eighteenths of a second (*ticks*) to that network.

DISPLAY SERVERS NetWare v2.2 and v3.11 console command that displays a list of file servers known to the bridge/router. Each file server is identified by a truncated file server name and the number of networks that must be crossed to reach the server (called *hops*).

distortion Unintended signal (waveform) changes during data transmission. Distortion can affect the wave's amplitude, attenuation (reduction in magnitude), peak phase, or harmonics or the beginning or ending of the signal.

distributed system Computer system designed to allow operation of software and applications on more than one machine. For example, a distributed database may reside partly on a

file server and partly on workstations.

DIX Type of multiple-pin plug and socket used to connect thick-Ethernet cabling to transceivers and network boards. DIX stands for Digital, Intel, Xerox— the three companies who developed the DIX protocol, a forerunner of the original Ethernet.

DLE See *data link escape.*

DMA See *direct memory access.*

DOS Operating system for IBM PC (PC DOS) and compatible (MS-DOS) computers.

NetWare workstations can use their own DOS files directly or copy DOS files and DOS directories into the NetWare SYS:PUBLIC directory. Use the MAP command-line utility to create a drive mapping; then add the drive mapping to the logic script.

A network supervisor or work group manager can create DOS directories with the USERDEF menu utility if users are being created at the same time.

DOS is also a NetWare console

command (v2.2) that allows nondedicated file servers and bridge/routers to function as local MS-DOS stations. To turn off the DOS mode, use the CONSOLE command.

DOS BREAK NetWare DOS BREAK ON login script command. A user can interrupt programs and DOS commands during login script execution by pressing <Ctrl><Break>. DOS BREAK OFF prohibits such interruptions.

DOS environmental variable Parameters that can be defined using the DOS SET (Set Environment) command. DOS variables, such as day_of_week or error_level, can be used in a NetWare login script if each variable is enclosed in "" (double quotes).

DOSGEN NetWare command-line utility that a supervisor can use to create a NET$DOS.SYS image file in a file server's SYS:LOGIN directory. Image files enable diskless and other workstations to boot from the server.

The network supervisor must first map a drive to the location of the im-

age file and add the drive mapping to the login script. The supervisor can then use DOSGEN to create the image file. NET$DOS.SYS should be flagged as Shareable/Read Only (SRO).

DOS ODI Novell Open Data-Link Interface software that allows various network protocols, such as TCP/IP, IPX/SPX, and AppleTalk to be used on a single network board. DOS ODI forms a "logical network board" that emulates various protocol configurations on the installed board. The logical network board operates as if physical boards were being used.

DOS SET NetWare login script command that permits setting of a DOS variable, such as day_of_week or error_level to be set to a specified value. The value must be enclosed within"" (quotation marks). DOS SET fills the function of the DOS SET command.

DOS VERIFY NetWare DOS VERIFY ON login script command automatically verifies the accuracy of data copied with the DOS COPY command.

DOS VERIFY OFF disables the automatic verification.

DOWN NetWare console command that automatically performs file and network functions in preparation for turning off the file server. DOWN saves file updates from the buffer, closes files, updates system records, and closes the operating system. The use of DOWN does not stop the reception of packets or the use of packet-oriented console commands such as TRACK ON and DISPLAY NETWORKS.

down command In NetWare v2.2, a utility issued from the command line of a server that is inoperative (down). Down commands are COMPSURF, DISKSET, and VREPAIR.

download To receive on a user's computer data sent to or retrieved from another computer, usually a more complex one. For example, a user could download a file from a mainframe to a workstation.

DOWNLOAD NetWare v2.2 utility, used during installation of a station on the

network, that copies configuration and linking files and file server utilities onto working diskettes.

drive A device that retrieves and loads computer data, from either a hard or fixed disk or a floppy diskette.

NetWare defines three groups of drives: **local drives**, designated by letters A through E; **network drives**, designated F through J (although all other letters of the alphabet may be used); and **search drives**, which are designated for file searches if the specified file is not in the current or active directory. Search drives are designated backwards through the alphabet, begining with the letter Z.

DRIVE NetWare login script command that specifies the letter or number of the drive that will automatically be presented to the user (default drive).

drive mapping Assigned connection between a directory and the logical network drive where it is located. The drive letter becomes part of the directory path so that a user can access network directories as easily as he or she scceses directories on local hard disk drives.

driver Hardware or software that connects an input/output device to a computer. A hardware driver amplifies a signal for long-distance transmission or sends it to many devices (fanout). It is also called a buffer/driver, bus driver, driver amplifier, or line driver.

A software driver is a program that connect an I/O device and a computer. In NetWare, a **disk driver** connects the operating system with the disk drives. Also, each network board requires a **LAN driver** loaded into the operating system. For example, 3C503.LAN is the LAN driver for an EtherLink II 3C503 network board (3COM).

driver amplifier See *driver*.

drop box directory or drop box folder A NetWare directory (v2.2, v3.11, Portable NetWare) or folder (NetWare for Macintosh) containing files that a user has the access rights to create, initially write to, and close, but does

not have the rights to open thereafter. On the Macintosh desktop, a drop box folder is gray with a black Down arrow.

DROUTER Portable NetWare utility that displays or prints a list of networks connected to the file server by network address, the number of networks that must be crossed to reach it (called *hops*), the amount of time required to transmit a packet in eighteenths of a second (*ticks*), and the address of the packet destination node.

This information is also available by selecting View/Print Router Table from the Transport Utilities Menu in SCONSOLE's Utilities Menu.

DSPACE NetWare v3.11 menu utility that allows a user to add or delete a file server attachment and restrict the size (in kilobytes) of the disk space assigned to a volume or a directory.

duplex Refers to data transmission modes. *Full duplex*, often called *duplex*, permits each end to send and receive data at the same time. In *half duplex*, each end can either send or receive data at one time, but cannot do both.

In NetWare, duplexing means copying a NetWare partition and data on a hard disk and duplicating it on several hard disks at the same time it is written on the original hard disk. Copying and duplicating a partition and data on a single hard disk is called mirroring.

DXMAID An IBM program used with all types of NetWare client drivers (both ODI and conventional) to create a CONFIG.SYS file when IBM LAN support is also used.

NETWARE DECODER

earth ground See *ground.*

EBCDIC (Extended Binary Coded Decimal Interchange Code) Eight-bit representations of letters, numbers, punctuation symbols, and control characters used on IBM and some other mainframe computers. EBCDIC has room for 256 entries, but not all bit combinations have been assigned.

echo check Method of data transmission error checking in which a receiving node transmits an incoming message back to the sender, so that it can be compared with the data as originally transmitted.

echo Signal distortion that reflects back to the sending node after a noticable time delay, causing interference. An echo can be suppressed by comparing signals going each way, then sending a distinct signal that disrupts the weaker of two similar signals, assumed to be the echo.

ECONFIG NetWare Ethernet CONFIGuration command-line utility used to configure stations and bridge/routers for either the IEEE standard 802.3 version of Ethernet, which is used by NetWare, or the Xerox Ethernet version, called Ethernet II. To configure the workstation shell, include the name of the IPX protocol file and the packet type with the ECONFIG command. In NetWare v2.2 and v3.11 use N for IEEE or E for Ethernet II. For example, using two disk drives, enter

```
A: ECONFIG B: IPX.COM:N
```
to select IEEE Ethernet.

In Portable NetWare, the Ethernet II designation is C.

ECONFIG can also be used to configure the bridge/router ROUTER.EXE file.

EDIF See *electronic design interchange format.*

EDIT NetWare v3.11 loadable module used for creation or editing

AUTOEXEC.NCF, STARTUP.NCF, and other batch files and text files. Use the LOAD EDIT command; then enter the path and, if editing a file, the file name. To save the change or new file, press Escape and answer Yes.

effective rights In NetWare, the security rights that a particular user has in a particular file or directory. In v2.2, effective rights are a combination of the user's already-granted trustee rights, those granted any group the user is part of , and the file or directorty rights that are active through the Maximum Rights Mask.

In v3.11 and Portable NetWare, a user's effective rights are determined by the previous directory level's effective rights and the current level's Inherited Rights Mask. Rights that are active in both of these levels (the intersection) will be the user's new effective rights unless any trustee rights have been granted. In that case, only the granted trustee rights will be the user's effective rights.

EIA (Electronic Industries Association) Trade association that sponsors numerous standards, such as the one for the RS-232C serial interface (now updated to EIA-232D). Other EIA-sponsored standards cover cabling, connectors, the Electronic Design Interchange Format (EDIF), data management, and testing.

EIA-232D Standard for serial communications that updates RS-232C.

eight-way splitter Network device that divides a signal into eight signals for transfer to and from eight stations. For example, an eight-way splitter can be used on an eight-station IBM PC broadband coaxial cable network. A network can contain several eight-way splitters.

electronic business data interchange (EDI) Standard data format used by many large corporations for network transmission of invoices, purchase orders, quotations, and other business documents. EDI supports both modem transmission and electronic mail. The name is often shortened to electronic data interchange.

electronic data interchange See electronic business data interchange.

electronic design interchange format (EDIF) Public domain data format for transmission of graphics, such as computer-aided design and electronic diagrams. EDIF describes boundaries, test patterns, logic symbols, ports, gate arrays, schematic diagrams, and layouts. It defines layers and provides device-size scaling information.

electronic mail (E-mail) Data transmission system in which messages are stored in a central system of "electronic pigeonholes" for retrieval by the recipient, rather than being received directly. Each user is assigned a unique address where messages originate and where they are received and stored for a given period of time. A password or other security method is employed. E-mail is usually implemented with special software that includes a text editor and methods of sending messages to one user, all users, or to a selected list of users.

One widely used TCP/IP protocol for E-mail is the Simple Mail Transfer Protocol (SMTP).

E-mail See electronic mail.

EMSNETx.EXE NetWare expanded memory shell file that places most of the NetWare shell in a workstation's expanded memory. The *x* refers to the station's version of MS-DOS, such as EMSNET4.EXE for DOS 4.0. The file is executed automatically when its name is included in the AUTOEXEC.BAT file.

emulation Ability of a network device to operate as a different type, such as a personal computer operating as a mainframe terminal or a network Medium Attachment Unit (MAU) of one type that works as another type, to connect different types of cabling.

ENABLE LOGIN NetWare (v2.2, v3.11) console command that restores users' ability to log in to a file server after access has been prevented with the DISABLE LOGIN command. In v3.11, ENABLE LOGIN also restores Supervisory access to an account that has been locked SYSCON when in-

truders were detected.

ENABLE TRANSACTIONS NetWare v2.2 console command that restores the Transaction Tracking System (TTS) after it has been disabled automatically by the file server (due to memory limitations) or manually with the console command DISABLE TRANSACTIONS.

ENABLE TTS NetWare v3.11 console command that restores the transaction tracking system (TTS) after it has been disabled automatically by the file server (due to memory limitations) or manually with the DISABLE TRANSACTIONS console command.

encapsulation Inclusion of transmission information in a message long with data. The information, such as sender's name and length of data, may be included in a header, which precedes the data.

encipher To put a message into private language; to code or encrypt. The term *encipher* is preferred internationally.

Restoring an enciphered message to plain language is called deciphering.

encode See *encrypt*.

encrypt To put data into code for security of the data or the system, for privacy and secrecy, or to assure its authenticity.

Data transmission can be encrypted at the sending node and decrypted at the receiving node, a method called *end-to-end*. If transmission is over a series of links, decryption and encryption can be performed at each intermediate node as well, a method called *linking*.

Public key encryption uses separate keys for encryption and decryption, one of which is known to the public.

One widely-used encryption system is the encryption/ decryption algorithm used by the U.S. government. It is defined in the data *encryption standard (DES)* and supported by the U.S. National Institute of Science and Technology. Another is RSA encryption (RSA Data Technology, Inc.).

In Portable NetWare, the SCONSOLE utility contains a Password Encryption Flag. When set to *active*, the flag encrypts passwords. The installed default, *inactive*, allows plain language (clear text) passwords. To set the flag, enter SCONSOLE Main Menu and select successively Configuration Menu, Services Configuration Menu, and Edit Security Parameters. NetWare v2.2 and v3.11 also support encrypted passwords.

ENDCAP NetWare END CAPture command-line utility. It reverses the effect of the CAPTURE utility, which takes data from an LPT port intended for a local printer and reroutes it to a remote printer. When issued without options, ENDCAP ends the capture of LPT1. To end the capture of a specified LPT port, use the Local option, as in the following example, which ends the capture of LPT3:

ENDCAP L = 3

End the capture of all ports with the ALL option.

The CANCEL (C) option ends the capture of LPT1 and deletes data without printing it. Cancel/Local ends the capture of any specified port and deletes the data without printing it, as in the following example:

```
ENDCAP C L = 3
```

Cancel ALL ends the capture of all ports and also deletes data without printing it.

This command is not to be confused with the CAPTURE *auto endcap* printing option. To print data after ENDCAP has been issued, the CAPTURE *auto endcap* and *timeout* options must be inoperative. The following command disables both options:

```
CAPTURE NA TI = 0
```

end of text (ETX) In data communications, a character indicating the end of a message or, in binary synchronous communication, the end of the last text block. ASCII uses the ETX control character (3 hexadecimal or decimal).

end of transmission (EOT) In data communications, a character indicating that transmission is complete. It is entered at the end of a message or at the end of the last message in a multiple-

message transmission. Afterwards, workstations revert to control mode, awaiting line activities such as token passing. ASCII uses the EOT control character (4 hexadecimal or decimal).

engine In general computer use, the command portion of an operating system or application that performs basic functions, such as retrieving and saving data. A database server is called an engine. *Engine* is also a synonym for the central processing unit (CPU).

In Portable NetWare, *engine* is synonymous with process, which in Unix terminology is one execution of a program by one user. For example, a network produces multiple NCP (NetWare Core Protocol) engines available for use. The SCONSOLE utility will spawn (create) a number of NCP engines (NWENGINES) beyond those in use, the number specified with the Spawn Ahead Processes parameter. Use the Edit File Services screen of the File Services Configuration Menu (selected from the SCONSOLE Services Configuration Menu). For example, specifying a number with the following token tells NetWare to create five more engines than are currently in use:

```
spawn_ahead_procs= 5 tells .
```

ENPS Component of the IPX/SPX protocol stack.

enquiry (ENQ) In data communications, a workstation's request for the identification or status of another station. For example, a workstation may ask another workstation whether it is ready to receive data. ASCII uses the ENQ control character (5 hexadecimal or decimal).

entry box NetWare screen display of a box in which a user can enter a parameter such as directory name or filename.

EOT See *end of transmission*.

Erase In NetWare, a user's right to delete a specified file or directory. The right can be granted to a user or it can be allowed as part of the Maximum Rights Mask (v2.2) or the Inherited Rights Mask (v3.11, Portable

NetWare). In versions of NetWare for Macintosh prior to v2.2, this right is known as *Delete*.

error detection In data transmission, the uncovering of data errors caused by the transmission process itself. Various methods are used, such as including parity bits, computing the value of the data bits as sent and comparing it with the value of the data as received, cyclic redundancy check (CRC), retransmission of the data back to the sender for comparison with the original, a check digit, or a checksum.

escape key Computer keyboard key used to negate a command or item selection. In NetWare, <Escape> is used to exit a submenu and return to its parent menu, to exit a utility menu and return to the utility prompt, or to continue a process.

Ethernet Set of cabling and connector specifications for transmission of data, voice, and video over local area networks (LANs) and metropolitan area networks (MANs). Ethernet provides a shared-medium, peer-to-peer topol-ogy that broadcasts to all workstations point-to-point with no intermediate switching node. Workstations transmit according to Carrier Sense Multiple Access/Collision Detection (CSMA/CD). Ethernet is patterned on the ISO/OSI reference model and is related to Layer 1, the physical layer, and to Layer 2, the Data-Link layer. Several variations are available, all but one transmitting at a rate of 10 megabits per second among workstations no more than 2.8 km (1.75 miles) apart.

Ethernet has two major types. One type is a direct descendant of the original protocol, called DIX, developed by Xerox Corp., Digital Equipment Corp., and Intel Corp. It is now often called **Ethernet II**. The other type has been developed under the auspices of the Institute of Electrical and Electronics Engineers (IEEE). It is usually called **Ethernet** or referred to by the IEEE standard number **802.3**.

IEEE Ethernet comes in six varieties. The four baseband varieties include *1BASE5*, a low-cost, limited distance configuration using twisted-pair wire that transmits at 1 megabit

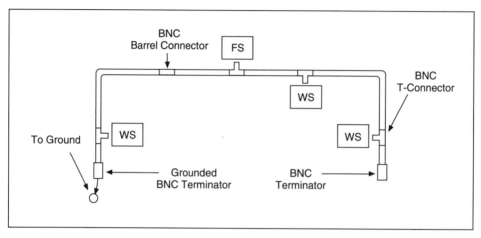

Shown are a thin-cable Ethernet layout (above) and a thick-cable layout (below).

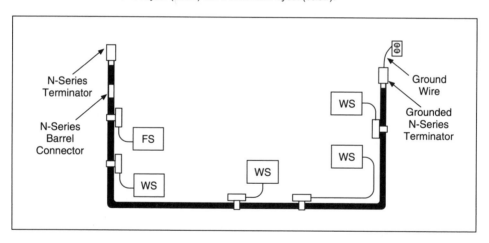

per second; *10BASE2*, a 10 Mb/s co-axial cable network often called **thin-Ethernet**; *10BASE5*, a 10 Mb/s coaxial cable network often called **thick-Ethernet;** and *10BASE-T*, a 10 Mb/s network using unshielded twisted-pair wire. *10BROAD36* uses CATV-type (community antenna or cable television) broadband coaxial cable. *FOIRL* (fiber optic inter-repeater link) uses fiber optic cable.

The two types of Ethernet differ principally in their packet frames, which are similar, but incompatible.

NetWare can be used with all varieties of Ethernet; however, all workstations on a network must use the same type, either Ethernet II or 802.3, if they are to communicate. NetWare software comes with 802.3 Ethernet as the default. To use Ethernet II with v2.2, run the ECONFIG command-line utility.

Ethernet II can be used with v3.11 by specifying it when installing the Ethernet LAN driver on the server, by running the PROTOCOL console command if a non-IPX protocol is desired, and by running the ECONFIG command-line utility on the worksta-tions and bridge/routers.

For Portable NetWare, use the NPSConfig file, *lan_<board network number>_packet_type = "<Ethernet type>"* token (the Ethernet type is either *802.3* or *ETHTYPE*). You must also use the ECONFIG utility to modify the LAN driver at the workstation.

ETHERRPL NetWare v3.11 ETHERnet Remote Program Load NLM that contains the protocol stack used to remotely boot a diskless IBM workstation that has Ethernet network boards installed. The process requires reconfiguring the boot files with DOSGEN and binding the protocol to the file server network boards. From ETHERRPL, enter the command:

```
BIND ETHERRPL
```

Include the name of the LAN driver.

The AUTOEXEC.NCF file must be similarly amended by adding the following commands:

```
LOAD ETHERRPL
BIND ETHERRPL
```

The commands must include the name of the LAN driver and any pa-

rameters currently being used.

ETX See *end of text*.

even parity See *parity*.

EVERYONE In NetWare v2.2 and v3.11, the name of a NetWare-created group to which all users of a file server are automatically assigned. The user receives these group rights: Create and Write rights to SYS:MAIL and Read and File scan rights to SYS:PUBLIC.

The network supervisor can assign users to other groups after the operating system has been installed.

execute only NetWare file attribute that prevents COM and EXE files from being copied or backed up. The attribute can be assigned only by someone with supervisory rights and cannot be revoked. Execute Only, abbreviated X, is assigned with the FILER menu utility.

EXIT NetWare login script command that ends execution of the script. To execute .COM and .EXE files and DOS internal commands or to use elec-

tronic mail, enter the command without options. To exit the login script and execute COMMAND.COM, also enter the filename.

To exit to electronic mail, include an IF...THEN login script command that sets the username parameter *%1* to equal the name of the E-mail system, as shown in the following example:

```
IF "%1" = "MAILNAME" THEN
EXIT "MAILNAME"
```

In v3.11, EXIT is a console command that returns a file server to DOS after its NetWare files have been closed with the DOWN console command. Issue the EXIT command after the DOWN command has been executed.

EXIT will also warm boot a file server from which DOS has been deleted with the REMOVE DOS console command.

expanded memory In MS-DOS and PC DOS, a computer memory management system that allows 32MB of memory located above the 1MB DOS limit to be used as if it were below the 1MB limit. Data that is located above

EE E E

1MB is copied into and removed from free memory below 1MB as needed. (This is defined as the LIM 4.0 specification.)

In NetWare v2.2 and v3.11, most of the shell can be moved into the expanded memory by using the Expanded Memory shell, located in the EMSNETx.EXE file (*x* stands for the version of DOS being used, such as EMSNET4.EXE for DOS 4).

A driver (not available with NetWare) must be installed for expanded memory to function.

(See illustration on following page.)

export To transmit data from one computer to another or from one application to another. The sender is the exporter and the receiver is the importer of the data.

extended memory In MS-DOS and PC DOS, computer memory above 1 MB. Extended memory requires special hardware and software. One widely available software interface is XMS, the eXtended Memory Specification (Lotus, Intel, Microsoft, and AST Research), which requires a device driver or XMM (eXtended Memory Manager).

In NetWare, most of the shell can be moved from conventional to extended memory by executing the XMSNETx.EXE file (*x* stands for the version of DOS being used, such as XMSNET4.EXE for DOS 4).

(See illustration on following page.)

EXTERNAL PROGRAM EXECU-TION NetWare login script procedure that permits an executable file (with the .COM or .EXE extension) to be run from within the LOGIN utility. Enter a # (pound sign), the path, and the name of the file. After execution, the login script is resumed.

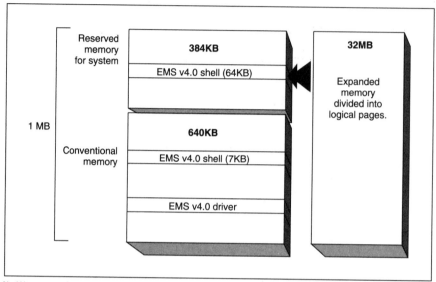

NetWare's expanded memory shell (above) takes about 7KB of conventional memory and loads the rest intoexpanded memory. The extended memory shell (below) requires 6KB and loads the remainder into extended memory.

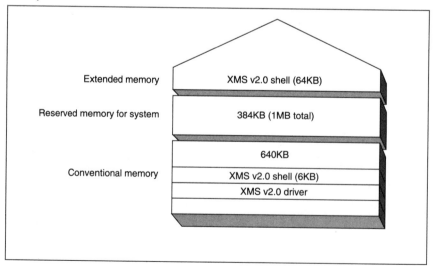

NETWARE DECODER

facsimile (FAX) Transmission of a signal derived from scanned text or a graphic image. The signal is reconstructed at the receiving end.

fake root In NetWare, the directory created to serve as a root directory for applications that must run on a root directory. With a search drive mapped to the fake root directory, the application can be accessed by users who have not been granted access rights to the actual root directory. The procedure is available with shell, expanded shell, and extended shell files using DOS 3.*x* or DOS 4.*x*.

FAT See *file allocation table*.

F-connector Network hardware connector similar to a cable TV connector. It is used, for example, as part of a base expander to connect an additional eight-way splitter and workstations to an IBM PC broadband coaxial cable network.

FCONSOLE NetWare menu utility that lets users change file servers and view the current version of NetWare and its user connections. FCONSOLE allows network supervisors to shut down the file server; it also allows network supervisors and file server console operators to alter the file server's status, disable the Transaction Tracking System (TTS), and broadcast messages.

FDDI See *fiber distributed data interface*.

FDISPLAY NetWare login script command that sends an ASCII file, including all control and escape characters, to network workstations and displays it when the workstations' users log in.

FDM See *frequency division multiplexing*.

fiber distributed data interface (FDDI) Protocol for using fiber optic cable in

communications networks, covering the Physical layer and the Data-Link layer of the ISO/OSI Reference Model. FDDI provides a packet-switched dual token ring network that transmits at 100 megabits per second. Up to 500 nodes can be connected to a 100 km (62 mi.) circumference network, with 2 km (1.6 mi.) between nodes.

Two classes of workstations are available. Class A workstations can be attached to both of the rings; class B workstations can be attached to one ring. A class B workstation can also connect to both rings through a star topology with a concentrator (hub).

FDDI is expected to become a series of American National Standards in 1992, including Physical layer medium-dependent, Physical layer protocol, media access control, and workstation management.

Several variations of FDDI are under development. One will send FDDI data over shielded or unshielded twisted-pair wire. FDDI-II, transmitting at 600 Mbps, will be a circuit-switched FDDI add-on for Integrated Services Digital Net-

works (ISDN) and PBX telephone systems.

fiber optic inter-repeater link (FOIRL) Type of IEEE Ethernet that uses fiber optic cable. The minimum medium propagation velocity of FOIRL is 0.66c (c = 3 x 108). Maximum cable segment length is 1,000 m with a maximum medium delay per segment of 5,000 ns.

fiber optics Transmission of data in the form of light pulses produced by a laser or light-emitting diode (LED) through glass fiber, plastic, or other dielectric (electrically nonconductive) material. Fiber optic transmission is generally considered baseband transmission.

Fiber optics provide high-speed transmission at low power. Fiber optics does not have crosstalk (signal interference), and optical signals carry much farther than other types carry before needing regeneration.

FIFO See *first in, first out.*

file The smallest independent unit of

stored information in a computer system. In a hierarchical data storage system, such as in MS-DOS or UNIX, a file is named and stored in a directory or subdirectory. In the Macintosh operating system, a file is stored in a folder.

NetWare stores the disk locations of files in the File Allocation Table (FAT).

In data management, a file is a collection of database records.

File Allocation Table (FAT) In NetWare, a volume file that records the disk locations of all data blocks. The FAT is loaded into a memory cache the file server uses to access data. Turbo FAT indexes the FAT locations of data files requiring more than 64 data blocks.

file attributes NetWare security attributes that can be set for a file using the FILER menu utility or FLAG command-line utility.

NetWare v2.2 uses the following file attributes: Archive Needed, Execute Only, Hidden (not listed in a directory scan), Indexed, Read Audit,

Read Only/Read Write, Shareable, System, Transactional, and Write Audit.

NetWare v3.11 uses the following file attributes: Archive Needed, Copy Inhibit, Delete Inhibit, Execute Only, Hidden, Purge, Read Audit, Read Only/Read Write, Rename Inhibit, Shareable, System, Transactional, and Write Audit.

Portable NetWare uses the following file attributes: Archive Needed, Copy Inhibit, Delete Inhibit, Execute Only, Hidden, Purge, Read Only/Read Write, Rename Inhibit, Shareable, and System.

file lock See *lock.*

File Mask Portable NetWare rights mask that prevents hybrid users from accessing their NetWare files through the host. The mask is a parameter of the SCONSOLE utility.

FILER NetWare menu utility used to view directory information, including owner, creation date and time, effective rights, directory attributes, rights in the Maximum Rights Mask (v2.2)

or Inherited Rights Mask (v3.11, Portable NetWare), and user or group trustees and rights. FILER can be used to modify directory information, including rights and attributes, user or group trustees, and trustee rights. Rights under the Mask can also be revoked or restored.

Only users with Supervisory rights are permitted to modify the directory's owner and creation date and time. Users with the appropriate rights can delete files and subdirectories, copy directories to other volumes, copy other subdirectories to the current directory, and copy a directory to another file server. Users can also move and copy files and change file rights. FILER options are selected from the Available Topics menu.

File Scan A NetWare file access right enabling a user to see a file name. As a directory right, File Scan allows a user to see a listing of a directory's files and subdirectories. The right can be granted to a user as a trustee right, or it can be part of a directory's rights under a Maximum Rights Mask (v2.2) or Inherited Rights Mask (v3.11, Portable NetWare). In NetWare for Macintosh v2.15, this right is called Search.

file server A computer that stores files and provides access to them for workstations. A computer can be used exclusively as a file server (dedicated); it can also be used as a workstation and a file server (nondedicated). In client/server architecture, some network operations are always handled by the file server.

In NetWare, a file server is controlled by a network supervisor or a designated file server console operator, who has been granted rights to monitor and control the file server and its use by workstations. Commands used to monitor and control the file server can be issued only from the console, a terminal connected directly to the file server.

In v2.2 and v3.11, the operating system runs on the file server. In Portable NetWare, the file server is a set of processes running on a host computer using the NetWare SCONSOLE utility as the network administrator's interface.

File Transfer Protocol (FTP) A protocol within TCP/IP that is based on TCP. FTP controls remote file retrieval, local file storage, storage of local files on remote servers, changes to different remote directories, and remote file deletion.

filter A routine that uses specified criteria to change data as it is transferred from one application to another or during a program operation. In UNIX, a filter reads input, transforms it, and writes it as output.

FIRE PHASERS NetWare login script command with which a user specifies how many times the "phaser" sound will be made upon login. A maximum of nine firings can be specified. For instance, to specify five firings, enter the following command:

    FIRE PHASERS 5 TIMES

first in, first out (FIFO) Queue or buffer organization that enters data and then removes the data in the order it was entered. FIFO is useful when the order of data in temporary storage must not be changed.

flag A marker or indicator, such as a marker for the end of a file or the end of a data word in data communications. Also a synonym for a Boolean variable.

For example, flags are used in the NetWare PSC (Print Server Command) command-line utility. PSC flags include abort, form feed, status, pause, and others. The Portable NetWare SCONSOLE utility sets many security flags.

In UNIX, a flag is an option that alters command execution.

FLAG NetWare command-line utility that displays a directory's file attributes and allows attributes to be changed.

FLAGDIR NetWare FLAG DIRectories command-line utility used to change subdirectory attributes in a given volume or directory. In v2.2, attributes are HELP, Hidden, Normal, PRivate, and SYstem. In v3.11 and Portable NetWare, subdirectory attributes are Delete Inhibit, HELP, Hidden, Normal, Purge, Rename Inhibit, and SYstem.

FM See *frequency modulation.*

FOIRL See *fiber optic inter-repeater link.*

form In NetWare, a screen window that includes fields which contain information that can entered or changed. A form may also include menu items that can be selected. Press <Enter> to move the cursor to the next field.

Form also means the type of paper specified for printing a document, defined for example in the PRINTDEF menu utility.

frame A data packet in Ethernet, token ring, and other network topologies. In asynchronous communication, a frame consists of a starting marker, the data, error-checking information, and an ending marker.

The two major types of Ethernet, IEEE 802.3 and Ethernet II, have similar but incompatible frames. Both frames contain headers identifying the destination, source, and length or type, followed by the data. However, the IEEE 802.3 length field is incompatible with the Ethernet II type field.

There are also variations of the IEEE 802.3 frame. (See illustration on opposite page.)

frame check sequence See *cyclic redundancy check.*

frequency division multiplexing Method of transmitting more than one high-speed signal at the same time by using a different frequency for each signal. In television transmission, frequency division multiplexing is used to send data and voice signals at the same time. A synonym is carrier system.

frequency modulation (FM) Method of transmitting an information signal by changing (modulating) the frequency of the carrier wave.

frequency shift keying (FSK) Frequency modulation technique for transmitting digital data, in which each of the two binary bit states (0 or 1) is represented by a predetermined frequency.

FSK See *frequency shift keying.*

FTP See *File Transfer Protocol.*

full duplex See *duplex.*

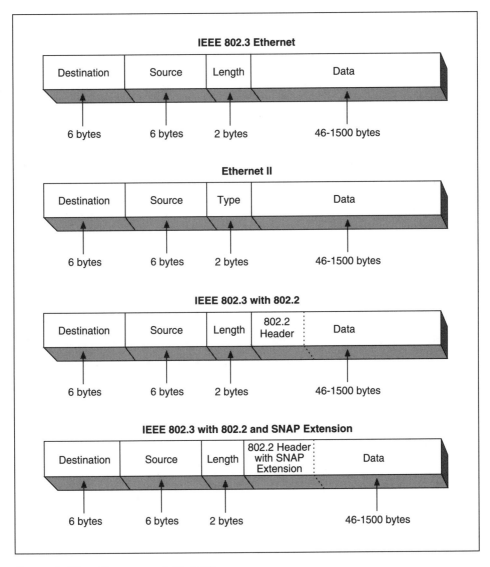

Here are the Ethernet frames supported by NetWare.

GG**G**G

NETWARE DECODER

gateway Connection between two different types of networks (such as a local area network and a wide area network), networks using different protocols, or a NetWare network and another type of network.

A gateway can be made up of a hardware node or software, or both. The connection may involve conversion between sending and receiving network protocols or between network protocols of the gateway and protocols of an internetwork or other intermediary network.

Gateways cover layers 4 through 7 (Transport through Application) of the ISO/OSI Reference Model.

GETLAN Portable NetWare command-line utility used by the network administrator to print or display on the screen a list of local area networks (LANs) attached to the file server. Information includes the network number and the node address.

GETLAN can also be selected as option 3 from the SCONSOLE Trans-port Utility Menu (accessed from the Main Menu and then the Utilities menu).

Gettydefs See *NVT*.

GOSIP United States Government Open Systems Interconnections Profile, a group of communications protocols used by agencies of the U.S. government.

GOTO A command used in some computer languages to execute a subroutine rather than the next line of code. In NetWare, GOTO is a login script command used to execute a script line or sequence out of order.

grace login A login permitted a user whose password has expired.

grant Permission given by a network supervisor to a user so that the user can access the network and specified directories and files on that network.

In NetWare v3.11 and Portable

GG GG

NetWare, a user can be assigned certain trustee rights to a file or a directory. In addition, access to directories can be limited with the Maximum Rights Masks (v2.2) or Inherited Rights Masks (v3.11, Portable NetWare). Which effective rights a person is granted depends on the limits of both types of access.

GRANT NetWare command-line utility that grants file or directory access rights to a user or a group (trustee rights). In v2.2, users must have the Access Control right to use the GRANT utility. A user with Access Control can grant Access Control, Create, Erase, File Scan, Modify, Read, and Write rights. The GRANT utility includes the ALL and N options: The ALL option grants all rights; the N option revokes all rights.

In v3.11 and Portable NetWare, a user with either Supervisory or Access Control rights can grant Access Control, Create, Erase, File Scan, Modify, Read, and Write rights. Only a user with Supervisory rights can grant the Supervisory right to another user.

When the ALL option is used, all rights are granted except the Supervisory right. The No rights option revokes all rights.

gray folder A desktop icon in NetWare for Macintosh that indicates a folder which the user cannot open. A user must be granted rights to open a particular folder.

ground To provide an electrical conductor to the earth or other very large body, in order to dissipate possibly damaging electricity that is extraneous to a system or a structure. For example, a lightning rod is a ground. A three-prong electric cord and wall socket provide an earth ground, as does a wire connected to a utility pipe that enters the ground.

In network hardware, some BNC terminators (thin Ethernet) and N-connectors (thick Ethernet) include grounding wires.

group In NetWare, a collection of users with the same rights. Every new user is automatically assigned to the group EVERYONE. A user with Supervi-

GG**G**G

sory rights can create new groups and assign users to them, add users to existing groups, and change the rights granted to a group.

guest A network device controlled by another network device (a host) during data transmission.

GUEST In NetWare, a temporary user of the network, assigned to the default group EVERYONE and granted its group rights, such as access to the PUBLIC directory and an electronic mailbox, and the Create right in the MAIL directory. If a network supervisor has granted other rights to EVERYONE, the guest also has those rights.

NETWARE DECODER

half duplex See *duplex*.

handshake or **handshaking** The first procedure in establishing a communications session. An example is the XON/XOFF asynchronous protocol, used in RS-232C serial communication.

hashing A search method in which a data storage address is a function value in a **hash table** that points directly to the file's disk location for quick, direct access. Hashing is also used for data security, in which the hash value depends in part on the date of data creation.

    In NetWare, the Hash table is located in cache memory.

HBA See *host bus adapter*.

HDLC See *High Level Data Link Control*.

header In communications, information included in a packet that precedes the data. The header can include the sender's name, transmission time, data length, and subject.

HELP NetWare (v2.2, v3.11, Portable NetWare) menu utility that provides online information about NetWare utilities, commands, and operations. To use, enter HELP and the name of a utility or command. You can also use the Scanning, File, and Display pull-down menus, with or without a mouse. Link tokens locate a word, phrase, or concept in different places within NetWare. Words and phrases can also be searched for. Boolean or conditional operators and wildcards can be used in searches. Information displayed from a HELP search can be saved in a file or printed.

    In NetWare Lite, the HELP screen is accessed by pressing F1.

hertz (Hz) Wave frequency or bandwidth measurement; 1 Hz equals 1 cycle per second.

heterogeneous Communications system composed of different types of hardware and a variety of protocols.

hexadecimal (hex) A number system with base 16, the system used for NetWare network addresses. The basic digits are 0, 1, 2, 3, 4, 5, 6, 7, 8, 9, A, B, C, D, E, and F.

hidden NetWare attribute that excludes the file or directory bearing it from a DOS directory scan. However, users with the File Scan right can see hidden files or directories with a NetWare NDIR scan.

High-Level Data-Link Control (HDLC) Internationally used protocol for serial, synchronous data transmission. HDLC performs the functions of layer 2, Data-Link, of the ISO/OSI Reference Model. It is a part of CCITT standard X.25.

holding time The time period used for each transmission on a channel.

HOLDOFF NetWare v2.2 command-line utility that closes a file kept open with

the HOLDON command-line utility.

HOLDON NetWare v2.2 command-line utility that allows a user to hold open a file in cases where the application does not automatically do so. This prevents others from using the file, but not from scanning it. HOLDON is cancelled by the HOLDOFF command-line utility.

home directory In NetWare, a directory that belongs to a single user. Home directories are created by the network supervisor. A login script drive mapping can provide immediate access to the home directory.

The NetWare for Macintosh equivalent is a *home folder*.

homogeneous A communications system that uses an integrated line of software and hardware.

horizontal parity See *parity*.

horizontal parity check See *longitudinal redundancy check*.

host In data communications, a device that controls another device (a *guest*)

during transmissions between the two. Traditionally, a host has been a mainframe computer that is accessed by terminals, printers, and other devices. In UNIX terminology, host means the computer that runs the operating system.

In Portable NetWare, the file server runs as a series of processes on the host computer, and NetWare users and host users are not always the same. Users who have the right to access NetWare files from the host are called *hybrid users*.

host bus adapter (HBA) In NetWare 2.2, a network board that identifies and controls communications between a file server and one or more external hard disk drives. An HBA is configured with the DISKSET command or an equivalent program.

An HBA is more commonly called a *disk coprocessor board* (DCB).

Hot Fix In NetWare, a method of preventing data from being written to bad data blocks on a hard disk. When a user saves data to the hard disk, the NetWare operating system verifies the save's accuracy by comparing the disk and RAM versions (*read-after-write verification*). If the two versions are not identical, the disk version is moved to a disk address known as the *Hot Fix Redirection Area*. The bad block address is stored in the operating system and no further data is written to it. (See illustration following.)

hub A central node or station through which other stations connect, used in star and ARCnet (including Novell RX-Net) topologies. A hub may perform multiplexing. Star network hubs are also called wiring closets or concentrators.

An RX-Net hub may be active or passive. An **active hub** can split a signal and amplify it, allowing it to be sent over longer distances. A **passive hub** is incapable of amplifying a signal.

HYBRID Portable NetWare utility the network administrator uses to assign a host user the right to access NetWare files. Such a user is called a *hybrid user*.

hybrid network Network that uses more than one topology and transmission method, such as a network with both a bus that uses multiple access and a ring employing token passing.

hybrid user In Portable NetWare, a user who has the right to access a NetWare file from the host. The network administrator can assign rights to be a hybrid user with the HYBRID utility. A user receives default access rights which are assigned in the NWConfig file. NetWare file rights can be withheld from a hybrid user by means of a file mask.

A hybrid user is added to the NetWare system through the SCONSOLE utility's Hybrid User Configuration Menu, which is accessed from the SCONSOLE Main Menu, through the Configuration Menu and the Services Configuration Menu.

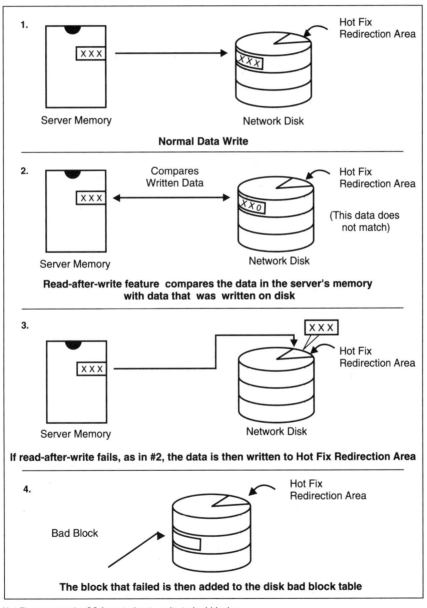

1.

Server Memory   Network Disk

Hot Fix
Redirection Area

Normal Data Write

2.

Compares
Written Data

Server Memory   Network Disk

Hot Fix
Redirection Area

(This data does
not match)

**Read-after-write feature compares the data in the server's memory
with data that was written on disk**

3.

Server Memory   Network Disk

Hot Fix
Redirection Area

If read-after-write fails, as in #2, the data is then written to Hot Fix Redirection Area

4.

Bad Block

Hot Fix
Redirection Area

The block that failed is then added to the disk bad block table

Hot Fix prevents the OS from trying to write to bad blocks

IBM$RUN.OVL NetWare overlay file, contained in the SYS:PUBLIC directory, that specifies color combinations for the screen palettes displayed on an IBM color monitor. The color combinations are available through the COLORPAL menu utility.

identifier The unique name or set of characters assigned to a user; also called a *user ID* or a *username*. The identifier must be entered into a computer or network before access is granted. An identifier is also the name or address of a workstation to which a data transmission is sent.

IEEE Institute of Electrical and Electronics Engineers, a professional society that sponsors numerous standards for network communications and other computer-related subjects. The IEEE 802.3 standard for Ethernet is an example.

IEEE 802.3 standard See *Ethernet*.

IF...THEN NetWare v2.2 login script command used for writing conditional statements that define the circumstances under which other commands will be executed. Such statements can include conditional symbols and Boolean operators, such as > (greater than), = (equal to), AND, and OR, as well as digits, day of the week, time of day, details of the network configuration and operating system, and other conditionals defined by the user.

IF...THEN..ELSE NetWare v3.11 and Portable NetWare login script command used for writing conditional statements that define the conditions under which other commands will be executed. Such statements can include conditional symbols and Boolean operators, such as > (greater than), = (equal to), AND,

and OR, as well as digits, day of the week, time of day, details of the network configuration and operating system, and other conditionals defined by the user.

impedance Measurement (in ohms) of the blocking of electrical current flow. It is the ratio of voltage to electrical current, and is composed of the portion of the flow that is dissipated (resistance) and the portion that is bound or stored (reactance).

Impedance varies with signal frequency. If a change in impedance occurs in a transmission path, part of the signal will be reflected in the opposite direction, causing a disruption.

import To receive a file or other data from another computer or application.

INCLUDE NetWare login script command that allows text files or other login scripts to be included in a user's logging in process. The script line should begin with the command, followed by the path and name of the file or script.

index A cross-reference of all entries in a computer file and their locations in the computer's memory. For example, database records can be indexed on one or more fields to permit flexible searches.

The NetWare Turbo FAT indexes files over 64KB. Turbo FAT contains the locations of a large file's data blocks in the File Allocation Table (FAT), which in turn lists the locations on the hard disk.

Indexed NetWare file security attribute, represented by I, that automatically adds File Allocation Table (FAT) listings of 64KB disk blocks to the Turbo FAT index for faster access.

Industry Standard Architecture (ISA) Standardized architecture for personal computers using an IBM AT bus or one that is compatible with it.

INFO NetWare Lite net info command that provides information about a workstation's CLIENT.EXE and (if loaded) SERVER.EXE files and the workstation's user.

inheritance Characteristic of hierarchical data structures and object- oriented programming that permits child or subordinate directories, files, and objects to have the same attributes as the parent from which they are derived.

In NetWare v2.2, a directory or file inherits rights that are set or altered in the Maximum Rights Mask of its parent directory or volume. Changes can also be made in individual subdirectories or files.

In NetWare for Macintosh, a user or group with trustee rights in a folder automatically inherits them for any nested folders later created in the original folder.

Inherited Rights Mask NetWare (v3.11, Portable NetWare) set of rights that applies to a file or directory when it is created. These rights are Access Control, Create, Erase, File Scan, Modify, Read, Supervisory, and Write. Rights in the mask apply automatically unless they are revoked by a user with Supervisory rights.

inset NetWare noninteractive screen that only displays information.

INSTALL 3.11, 2.2 NetWare v2.2 program and v3.11 loadable module used to install, modify, or update the NetWare operating system. The v2.2 program consists of four modules, selected from a main menu, that do the following: generate the operating system, including configuring LAN drivers and disk drivers; link and configure the operating system and file server utilities; perform a track zero test on a hard disk; and incorporate name, volume, and partition information in the file server.

The v3.11 module (contained in the INSTALL.NLM file) is loaded with the LOAD console command. All commands can be selected from a main menu. INSTALL contains the commands for installing or replacing hard disks, partitioning and modifying hard disks, mirroring (copying a partition from one disk to another) or unmirroring hard disks, formatting hard disks, and executing the surface test to find bad blocks on hard disks. INSTALL also creates volumes, cre-

ates the AUTOEXEC.NCF and STARTUP.NCF network startup files, and installs file server products.

Integrated Services Digital Network (ISDN) Communications network that uses digital telephone lines for simultaneous transmission of data, video, and voice.

interface In data communications, a connection between a computer and another device, or between two devices. Electrical and mechanical components and software may be included. The RS-232C serial communications standard is an example.

INT2F.COM Novell Open Data-Link Interface (ODI) file. This file is used by workstations (whose applications require NETBIOS.EXE) to communicate with a NetWare file server.

internetwork A network composed of a backbone and many different kinds of local, metropolitan, and wide area networks. For example, NSFNET, a network operated by the U.S. National Science Foundation, connects many university and research institution networks. NSFNET, in turn, is a participant in Internet, an internetwork operated by the U.S. Department of Defense. See illustration on next page.

Internetwork Packet Exchange See *IPX.*

interoperability The operating compatibility of many different types of network devices and software for transmitting and receiving data communications. For example, the ISO/ OSI Reference Model and widely used protocols such as NetWare IPX/SPX, TCP/IP, and the U.S. government's GOSIP protocol collection provide interoperability. The NetWare Open Data-Link Interface (ODI), which allows one network board to handle multiple protocols and LAN adapters, is another example of interoperability.

International Organization for Standardization (ISO) International organization that sponsors many standards related to data communications, including the ISO/ OSI Reference Model. The American

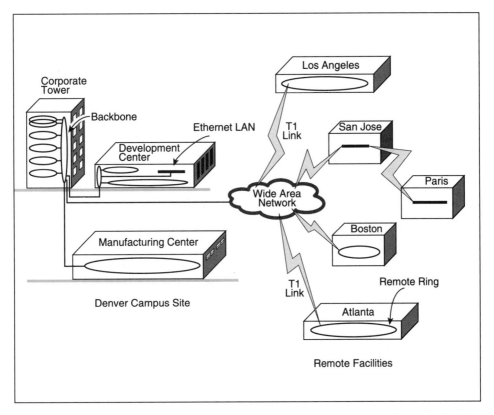

An example of an internetwork; here the backbone is a ring topology, which is connected to other local and wide area networks.

National Standards Institute is a member of ISO. ISO works closely with CCITT.

Inter-Process Communication (IPC) In Portable NetWare, communication among the NetWare processes running on the host, including tracking user accounts, drive mappings, logins, and other information. The size of the memory block devoted to these activities is set in the SCONSOLE Edit System Parameters screen (select Shared Memory Size). This screen is entered from the Configuration menu in the SCONSOLE Main Menu. The amount of host time devoted to IPC can be set by selecting Priority on the screen, and entering a number from 0 through 40.

interrupt A communications signal from a device or software that suspends an ongoing computer process and requires action on the signal. When the action is completed, the computer resumes its previous operation. The interrupt signal can be sent automatically because of a device's internal condition, or it can be entered from a keyboard. For example, pressing <Ctrl><C> produces an interrupt. Usually each network device has a unique interrupt signal.

I/O channel An input/output channel, either a hardware path or a frequency for data communication.

IP (Internetwork Protocol) Communications protocol that is part of a series of protocols called TCP/IP. The function of IP covers Layer 3, Network, of the ISO/OSI Reference Model. IP prepares datagram packets for communication between the Data-Link/Physical layers using Ethernet, Token Ring, or other topologies, and the Transport/Session layers, composed of TCP or UDP. It adds a packet header that includes the sender's and receiver's addresses and the addresses of intermediate computers. IP inspects incoming packet checksums for transmission integrity and discards packets with inaccuracies.

IPC See *Inter-Process Communication.*

ipc_access A configuration parameter in the NWConfig file.

IPX NetWare Internetwork Packet eXchange protocol, used along with SPX as the resident protocol in NetWare. IPX is installed as an **IPX driver** under the **IPX.COM** filename and configured with WSGEN (v2.2, v3.11), SHGEN (Portable NetWare), or ECONFIG. IPX receives data packets from the NetWare shell, adds addresses and routing information to outgoing packets, and then transmits the packets through the LAN driver and network board. IPX routes incoming packets to the addressed node.

In v3.11, **IPX** is the name of a command line utility used to see the version and options of IPX.COM. It can also be used to change the network board's configuration number without using DCONFIG.

IPXODI.COM NetWare file containing the IPX protocol stack for use with the Open Data-Link Interface, allowing workstations to communicate with NetWare file servers.

IPXS NetWare v3.11 loadable module for use with other modules, such as CLIB (C library), that require the STREAMS IPX module services.

IPX/SPX Series of modules and drivers that comprise the resident protocols in NetWare, *IPX* and *SPX*.

ISA See *Industry Standard Architecture*.

ISDN See *Integrated Services Digital Network*.

ISO See *International Organization for Standardization*.

ISO/OSI Reference Model A model protocol approved by the International Organization for Standardization (ISO standard 7498) to provide an Open Systems Interconnection (interoperability) for data communications. The model has seven layers:

Layer 7, Application layer, is the network/application interface.

Layer 6, Presentation layer, translates messages between the network software's format and an international standard format used for transmission.

Layer 5, Session layer, determines communications paths for a transmission.

ISO/OSI Model
Layers

Application	
Presentation	Service Protocols
Session	
Transport	Transport Protocols
Network	
Data Link	Media Access Protocols
Physical	

The ISO/OSI reference model for communication shows how computers communicate through layered protocol stacks.

Layer 4, Transport layer, assures the reliability of the data being transmitted.

Layer 3, Network layer, moves data packets between the network and Layer 4.

Layer 2, Data-Link layer, formats outgoing data packets for transmission and makes sure they are received correctly. This layer also checks incoming packets to determine if they are intended for the local workstation.

Layer 1, Physical layer, carries the incoming and outgoing unformatted data.

NETWARE DECODER

jumpers Network board pins that are connected during board configuration.

JUMPERS NetWare (v2.2, v3.11) menu utility for adding options to jumpers-configurable IPX LAN drivers, to match board settings for either an ISA workstation with dedicated IPX or an 80286-based file server or bridge/router. Supervisor rights are required to use this utility.

NETWARE DECODER

Kermit Byte-count protocol for asynchronous communications between personal computers, over telephone lines, and between personal computers and mainframes. A Kermit packet consists of a header containing length, sequence, and other control information, followed by the data. The packet ends with a check character consisting of the sum of all preceding characters. Kermit sends packets in sequences numbered 0-63 and then begins again with 0 (modulo 64). If the receiving station does not acknowledge receipt, the sender retransmits.

NETWARE DECODER

LAN See *local area network.*

LAN driver Software that establishes communication between a file server's network board and the NetWare operating system. NetWare provides the TRXNET.LAN driver for ARCnet boards; 3C503.LAN, 3C505.LAN, 3C523.LAN, NE2.LAN, NE232.LAN, NE1000.LAN, NE2000.LAN, and NE3200.LAN drivers for Ethernet boards; the PCN2.LAN driver for IBM PC Network boards; and the TOKEN.LAN driver for Token-Ring boards. Third-party drivers are also available.

In v2.2, a LAN driver is loaded from the LAN_DRV_*xxx* diskette during network installation or upgrading with INSTALL. In v3.11, a driver is loaded at the file server with the LOAD *LAN driver* module. For a client, a driver is loaded with SHGEN or WSGEN (select a driver from the LAN Driver Op-

tions menu or from the LAN_DRV_??? diskette).

language In Portable NetWare, a token in the NWConfig file defining the language used for system messages. English is the installation default.

LANSUP.COM NetWare driver on workstations using the IBM LAN Support Program for Token-Ring or PC-Net networks. The driver is in the ODI directory.

library A collection of computer routines or modules of code or functions in executable form, available for frequent use. For example, in NetWare v3.11, the CLIB loadable module is a library of C routines.

line See *channel.*

line driver See *driver.*

link A pointer between elements of a queue, stack, or other data structure.

For instance, link tokens in NetWare online HELP display related information from different parts of the system.

A linked list is an ordered list of elements. The list includes pointers to other elements.

The Data-Link layer (layer 2 of the ISO/OSI Reference Model) prepares outgoing data in packets or frames and includes an error-checking method. The Link Support Layer (LSL) in the NetWare Open Data-Link Interface (ODI) performs a similar function.

In data communications security, link refers to a system where encryption and decryption are performed at the beginning and ending nodes and at each intermediate node.

LINK DRIVER Open Data-Link Interface (ODI) command in the NET.CFG file used to enter the name of a LAN driver.

Link Support Layer (LSL) Open Data-Link Interface (ODI) software implementation on a workstation. LSL

functions between the LAN driver and IPX, TCP/IP, or other communications protocol.

LSL.COM is a NetWare program file used for communication between the device driver (LAN driver) and IPX on the client station.

list In NetWare, a series of selectable items similar to a menu. Items can be added to or removed from some lists.

LISTDIR NetWare command-line utility that lists a directory's Maximum Rights Mask (v2.2) or Inherited Rights Mask (v3.11, Portable NetWare), a user's effective rights in the directory, the name of each subdirectory, and the date or time the subdirectory was created.

LOAD NetWare (v3.11) console command that loads NetWare Loadable Modules, including disk and LAN drivers, name space (for storing non-DOS files), and NLM utilities.

For disk drivers, LOAD may be used to load an ISADISK or DCB driver into an Industry Standard Architecture (ISA) controller (either AT

or Novell SCSI). This module can also be used to load a PS2ESDI, PS2MFM, or PS2SCSI into ESDI, MFM, or IBM SCSI microchannel controller. An ISADISK or proprietary driver can be installed in an Extended Industry Standard Architecture (EISA) AT or proprietary controller. The command is also used for upgrading and troubleshooting.

For LAN drivers, LOAD is used to install a LAN driver and link it to a file server's network board. The module is used to load the TRXNET.LAN driver for ARCnet boards; 3C503.LAN, 3C505.LAN, 3C523.LAN, NE2.LAN, NE232.LAN, NE1000.LAN, NE2000.LAN, and NE3200.LAN drivers for Ethernet boards; the PCN2.LAN driver for IBM PC Network boards; and the TOKEN.LAN driver for Token-Ring boards. The command is also used for upgrading and troubleshooting.

loadable module See *Netware Loadable Modules*.

local area network (LAN) A communi-cations network that is confined to a single building or site, usually with a maximum distance of no more than 2,000 to 7,000 feet (600 to 2,100 m). This type of network is used in an office or department. A LAN can be connected to other similar LANS, to LANs of different speeds or levels of traffic, to metropolitan area networks (MANs, which are similar to LANs, but cover a greater distance), and wide area networks (WANs). LANs can be connected by gateways, bridges, or routers. LANs can use coaxial cable, twisted-pair wire, or fiber optic cable, and baseband or broadband frequencies. Computers and peripheral devices may be connected in bus, ring, or star topologies.

Stations can communicate with such methods as contention, carrier sense multiple access (CSMA), token passing, or polling. Widely used network specifications include Ethernet and ARCnet. NetWare is an operating system for local area networks.

lock Exclusive ownership or use of a workstation, system, directory, or

file that prevents others from using it. Locks are placed for security purposes, in order to prevent multiple users from making changes simultaneously, or to assure that each user has the most recent version. In some cases, a lock is placed on part of a file, but not all of it. A locked file can be scanned but not changed by others. Locks are placed by applications and programs. NetWare manages locks for network operations.

In NetWare, a **file lock** locks an entire file. A **record lock** locks a database record for the time period it is in use. (See illustration on opposite page.) *Semaphores* lock files while the files are in use.

A **physical lock** locks part of a shared file by defining a range of locked bytes. A **logical lock** defines and controls user access to various parts of a shareable file.

In NetWare v2.2, a file's lock information is displayed with the FCONSOLE utility. Use the File/Lock activity screen to select either Logical Lock Information or File/Physical Records Information. You can also use the Connection Information screen to select either Logical Record Locks or Physical Records Locks (select Open Files/Physical Records first).

In NetWare v3.11, the network conditions under which locks are handled are defined with the SET console command.

To see the lock status of a Portable NetWare file, select the Statistics Menu from the SCONSOLE Main Menu. The File Lock Statistics screen displays the number, requests, and maximum simultaneous logical and physical locks and semaphores. An ACTIVE *Native Locks* parameter, set in SCONSOLE, applies locks to both NetWare and the host operating system. INACTIVE locks only within NetWare.

Release of the exclusive ownership or use is called **unlocking**.

log A record of occurrences, such as a network's logins and other transactions. In NetWare, a chronological list of each login and logout of a network is stored in the file NET$ACCT.DAT and can be displayed and printed with the PAUDIT command-line utility.

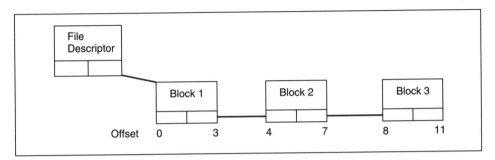

This is a simple 12KB file consisting of three 4KB blocks.

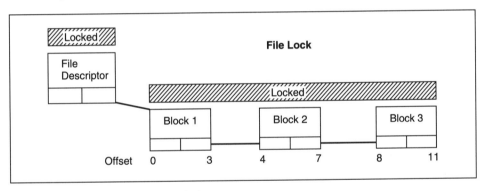

A file lock results in the entire file being locked.

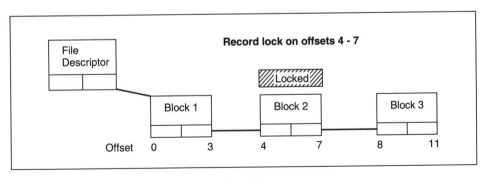

With record locking, only a portion of the file is locked at a time.

logical According to reason or logic, independent of the restrictions of the physical environment. For instance, a logical network topology is the theoretical configuration, which is embodied in the physical topology. The physical topology is the actual arrangement of nodes and wiring.

logical address See *address*.

logical lock See *lock*.

logical network See *network*.

logical topology See *topology*.

login/log in To enter a network; to begin a session; to make contact with another network node. Depending on the computing environment, the phrase is log in, log on, or login. NetWare favors *log in*. The NetWare login process is contained in a user's login script.

To leave a network or terminate a session is to **log off** or **log out**.

LOGIN NetWare command-line utility whose execution logs a user into the network. The login process is de-

fined in a set of commands called the **login script**. Some commands are included in a system script, written by the network supervisor. Each user can also write a script using the SYSCON menu utility (select the User Information option from the Available Topics menu). A user's login script can be modified; the current version of a user's login script is stored in the user's electronic mail box.

NetWare v2.2 uses the following login script commands: #, ATTACH, BREAK, COMSPEC, DISPLAY, DOS BREAK, DOS SET, DOS VERIFY, DRIVE, EXIT, EXTERNAL PROGRAM EXECUTION, FDISPLAY, FIRE PHASERS, GOTO, IF...THEN, INCLUDE, MACHINE, MAP, PASSWORD EXPIRES, PAUSE, PCCOMPATIBLE, REMARK, SHIFT, and WRITE.

NetWare v3.11 uses the following login script commands: #, ATTACH, BREAK, COMSPEC, DISPLAY, DOS BREAK, DOS SET, DOS VERIFY, DRIVE, EXIT, FDISPLAY, FIRE PHASERS, GOTO, IF...THEN...ELSE, IN-

CLUDE, MACHINE, MAP, PAUSE, PCCOMPATIBLE, REMARK, SHIFT, and WRITE.

Portable NetWare uses the following login script commands: #, ATTACH, BREAK, COMSPEC, DISPLAY, DOS BREAK, DOS SET, DOS VERIFY, DRIVE, EXIT, FDISPLAY, FIRE PHASERS, GOTO, IF...THEN...ELSE, IN-CLUDE, MACHINE, MAP, PAUSE, PCCOMPATIBLE, REMARK, SHIFT, and WRITE.

SYS:LOGIN is a directory created by the NetWare operating system when a network is installed. The directory contains the LOGIN utilities, contained in the LOGIN.EXE executable file and SLIST.

log off See *log out.*

log on See *login.*

log out To terminate a communications session. To exit a network to which one has logged in. Sometimes called **log off**.

LOGOUT NetWare (v2.2, v3.11, Portable NetWare) command-line utility with which a user closes communication with one or more file servers. To use, enter the command, followed by the name of the server.

In NetWare Lite, users can use the following command to exit the network:

```
net logout
```

longitudinal parity check See *longitudinal redundancy check.*

longitudinal redundancy check (LRC) Method of data transmission error-checking in which the check character is the accumulation of exclusive-OR bit values of the characters transmitted. The check character is sent at the end of the block. When the block is received, the character is reaccumulated and compared to the character as sent. If the two are unequal, a transmission error has occurred.

An LRC is also called a longitudinal parity check or a horizontal parity check.

long machine name or **type** A network

station's name in MS-DOS or PC-DOS, consisting of no more than six characters, such as IBM_PC. It is entered in a NetWare login script with the command MACHINE.

loop An endless configuration, such as a circle. In programming, a loop is a routine whose last line returns to the first line.

In network and data communications, a closed circuit or transmission path. In network configuration, a cable that passes from its hub of origin to other hubs and then back to the original hub.

lost packet resends In Portable NetWare, a parameter displayed on the SCONSOLE File Server Statistics screen (available through the SCONSOLE Main Menu and the Statistics Menu). If a large number of retransmissions occur because packets were not received by clients, a hardware or software problem may exist at either end.

LPT1, LPT2, LPT3 Name usually given to first, second, and third parallel ports on IBM PC and compatible computers.

LRC See *longitudinal redundancy check*.

LSL.COM See *link support layer*.

LU 6.2 Logical Unit 6.2, the IBM protocol within Advanced Program-to-Program Communications (APPC) for terminal-to-mainframe communications. It covers Layer 5, the Session layer, of the ISO/OSI Reference Model. It is also used in IBM Systems Network Architecture (SNA).

MACHINE NetWare login script command that specifies the workstation's long machine name as assigned in SHELL.CFG or NET.CFG. The command is required in order to run NetBIOS.

machine name A workstation's name in MS-DOS. A machine has a **long machine name** or **type** of no more than six characters, such as IBM_PC. It is assigned in the SHELL.CFG or NET.CFG file and can be entered in a NetWare login script with the MACHINE command.

A **short machine name** or **type** has no more than four characters, such as IBM, and is used in NetWare overlay files (.OVL extension), such as CMPQ$RUN.OVL, to determine screen palette colors. The short machine name is identified as SMACHINE.

MACINST NetWare for Macintosh diskette and program used to install the MACSETUP installation and configuration program.

MAC.NAM NetWare v3.11 file that enables a file server to be a NetWare for Macintosh target file server. After entering the LOAD MAC command, enter the INSTALL command, which permits editing of the STARTUP.NCF file.

Use the ADD NAME SPACE console command to add directory space to a volume so that it can store Macintosh files.

MACSETUP NetWare for Macintosh program for installation and configuration, run after MACINST. A network supervisor logged into a NetWare file server through a DOS client must perform the MACSETUP procedure, which consists of installing a hidden Desktop folder in each volume in up to eight target file servers, creating AppleTalk print queues. NetWare for Macintosh is also installed on an external router.

MAIL NetWare directory that provides electronic mail boxes. MAIL is automatically created in the SYS volume when the network is installed. It contains a subdirectory for each user that serves as a mailbox that uses the user's ID as an address. The subdirectory also contains the user's login script. Each user is automatically granted the Create directory right.

maintenance, network Ongoing activities that ensure efficient performance of hardware and software. The NetWare operating system provides numerous error, warning, and status messages that are displayed on the screen as conditions warrant. In addition, the network administrator or (in some cases) users can perform maintenance tasks such as backing up volumes, data files, and the Bindery, monitoring memory pools, buffers, and file service processes, and regulating and testing security procedures to prevent unauthorized entry and data corruption.

MAKEUSER NetWare menu utility that a network supervisor or workgroup manager uses to add and remove network users. A USR file is created for each individual or group user. The file can be written within MAKEUSER or as an ASCII/DOS file using a text editor or word processing program.

Each file must contain either the #CREATE or #DELETE keyword and the user's name. CREATE may include the user's full name, password, group name, and directory rights. The following keywords can also be used: #ACCOUNTING, #ACCOUNT_EXPIRATION (only if #ACCOUNTING is also used), #CLEAR or RESET (to start a new set of keywords in the same file, such as a group user file), #CONNECTIONS (number of concurrent connections), #GROUPS, #HOME_DIRECTORY (path), #LOGIN_SCRIPT, #MAX_DISK_SPACE (number of blocks assigned), #NO_HOME_DIRECTORY (v2.2 only), #PASSWORD_LENGTH (number of characters), #PASSWORD_PERIOD (number of days it is valid),

#PASSWORD_REQUIRED, #PURGE_USER_DIRECTORY (when a user is deleted), #REM, #RESTRICTED_TIME (time periods when the user is not allowed to access the file server), #STATIONS (the stations the user can use to log in), and #UNIQUE_PASSWORD.

MAKEUSER is similar to the USERDEF menu utility, which uses a template instead of a USR file.

MAN See *metropolitan area network.*

managed users and groups In NetWare, a SYSCON User Information menu item containing the names of managed users and groups—those whose accounts are controlled by an account manager. The menu information can be changed by a network supervisor or user account manager.

manager See *user account manager; workgroup manager.*

managers In NetWare, a SYSCON User Information Menu item used to manage the name of a user or workgroup manager. The menu information can

be changed by a network supervisor or user account manager.

map A graphical representation of a network, cable, or segment.

A **map** or **mapping** is the transferring of data between a disk and a computer's RAM. In NetWare, it is the assigning of a drive letter to a path from a station to a volume or directory on a file server. When the drive letter is entered at the command line, the volume or directory is automatically active. A drive mapping is performed on a one-time basis with the MAP command-line utility or saved for future use with the MAP login script command.

MAP NetWare command-line utility and also a login script command. The utility is used for creating, viewing, or changing drive mappings, creating or changing search drive mappings, and mapping a drive to a fake root directory or to the next available drive.

Drive mappings expire when the user logs out unless they have been

saved in the user's login script with the MAP command. A drive can be mapped to a specified directory or to a directory with another drive mapping. A search drive can be inserted into a search drive sequence and a drive can be mapped to a fake root directory.

mark key Use of the F5 key in NetWare to mark multiple list items.

master See *host*.

MATHLIB NetWare v3.11 MATH LIBrary loadable module to be used with the CLIB loadable module on a server with an 80387 math coprocessor or 80486 processor.

MATHLIBC NetWare v3.11 MATH LIBrary C loadable module to be used with the CLIB loadable module on a server that does not have a math coprocessor).

Maximum Rights Mask NetWare (v2.2) set of rights that applies to a directory when it is created. These rights are Access Control, Create, Erase, File Scan, Modify, Read, and Write. Rights in the mask apply automatically unless they are revoked by a user with Supervisory rights. Changes in a directory's mask affect the masks of subdirectories.

MEMORY NetWare v3.11 console command that shows how much computer memory the NetWare operating system is currently addressing. The maximum on ISA (AT bus) and microchannel computers is 16MB, unless the REGISTER MEMORY console command is used to make higher memory address available. For EISA computers, memory above 16MB is automatically used through the SET console command.

memory pool In NetWare, the method of managing Random Access Memory (RAM) in which memory not used by the operating system is kept in a pool. Memory from this pool can be assigned for other use or withdrawn as required. Part of the pool is used for file caches (buffers) for often used files, such as loadable modules and the File Allocation Table (FAT).

The permanent part of the pool is used for caches that are occupied for a longer period of time, such as holding directories or incoming packets. Alloc memory pool holds network services, such as drive mappings, queue management, messages awaiting broadcasting, and user connections.

memory, shared   In Portable NetWare, virtual memory in the host used for interprocess communication (IPC). The size of shared memory and the shared memory *key* (which assigns a memory area to IPC) are set with the SCONSOLE Edit System Parameters screen, via the Main Menu and the Configuration Menu.

memory, virtual Method of increasing the apparent size of a computer's RAM by temporarily moving some of its data to disk storage to make room for new data. The process of moving data between disk and RAM is called *swapping*.

menu A screen list of executable options. Many NetWare commands and utilities are menu oriented. A NetWare

menu utility is accessed by entering its name at the prompt. The main menu of the utility presents options for submenus.

NetWare also allows users to create custom menus that can be accessed with the MENU menu utility.

MENU NetWare menu utility that allows users to use customized menus created as ASCII files with a text editor or word processor. The menu may contain, for example, the commands to open files and applications, manipulate a subdirectory, and execute utilities. The user can also design the menu's screen appearance and colors. To use the menu, enter MENU and the menu name, including the extension (unless the extension is .MNU).

message A unit of communication between stations or processes, with a beginning, content, and an ending. A message can be composed of a single packet or a series of packets.

message packet See *packet*.

message system IPX-compatible communications protocol used to broadcast messages among network nodes. In NetWare, the message system is used to broadcast file server messages to network supervisors and workgroup managers.

metropolitan area network (MAN) Communications network with many of the characteristics of a local area network, but covering a larger geographical area. For example, the IEEE Ethernet specifications are applicable to a MAN as well as a LAN.

Micro Channel architecture Proprietary computer architecture for the IBM PS/2 series, designed for multiprocessing. It uses built-in ESDI and MFM controllers and either a built-in SCSI controller or an IBM SCSI adapter. NetWare provides PS2ESDI.DSK, PS2MFM.DSK, and PS2SCSI.DSK disk drivers for Micro Channel workstations.

mirror In NetWare (v2.2, v3.11), to copy a hard disk's NetWare partition and data and duplicate it on another hard disk (called a *secondary disk*) at the same time it is written on the original disk (*primary disk*). Mirroring is set up during installation. In v2.2, select Mirror Status from the File Server Definition screen. In v3.11, select Mirroring from the INSTALL loadable module's Available Disk Options menu, via the Installation Options menu and the Disk Options menu.

When the partition and data are duplicated across disk channels, the process is called *duplexing*. (See illustration on following page.)

mixed network A network with servers using different versions of NetWare.

modem A MOdulator-DEModulator; a device for sending computer data over telephone lines by translating signals between a computer's digital data and a telephone line's voice (analog) data. The modem modulates outgoing computer signals and demodulates incoming analog signals.

In network security, a **call-back modem** intercepts an incoming telephone call and requests access infor-

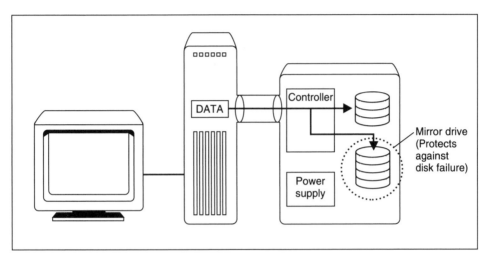

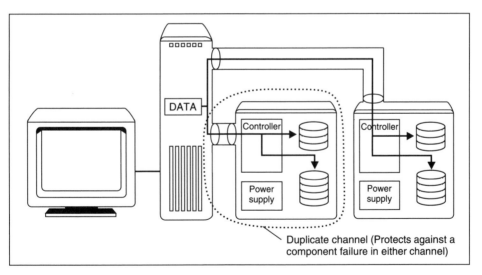

Disk mirroring (above) and disk duplexing (below) prevent data loss.

mation, including a password. If the information is verified, the modem instructs the caller to hang up and then allows access to the user by calling the user at a previously identified telephone number.

Modify NetWare security right that allows users to change the attributes and names of directories or files. The Modify right at the directory level also applies to the directory's files. In v3.11, the specified right can also be granted for a specified file.

modulate To change a carrier wave so that it can transmit data. The wave's amplitude (AM), frequency (FM), or phase (PM) can be changed.

module In Portable NetWare, a parameter in the SCONSOLE Edit Network Assignments menu, via the Main Menu, Configuration menu, and Transport Configuration menu. The menu is used to identify network boards. Module adds any required data parsing for the particular board and network specifications.

module, loadable See *loadable module*.

MODULES NetWare v3.11 console command used to display the short and long names of modules and the version number of NLMs loaded on a file server.

MONITOR NetWare v2.2 console command for tracking station status, logins and logouts, file use and status (such as whether the file is locked), and operating system characteristics (such as number of buffers).

In v3.11, MONITOR is a loadable module used to list connections, locks, and open files; provide hard disk and LAN information; list modules and the resources they use; lock and unlock the console; and describe the file server memory and its use. See illustration next page.

MOUNT NetWare (v2.2, v3.11) console command used to make a volume available to users. MOUNT can be used for a newly created volume or one that has been made inactive with the DISMOUNT console command. To make a single volume available, fol-

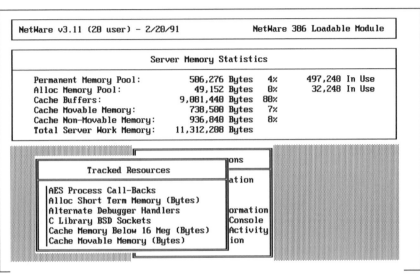

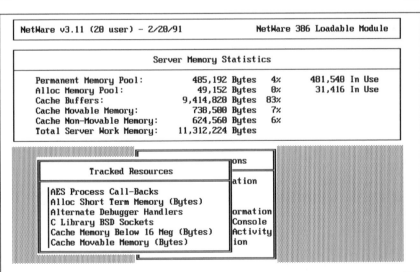

MONITOR can be used for such purposes as displaying how much memory is being used in each of NetWare's memory pools (above) or displaying list of "Tracked Resources" that can be investigated (below).

low the command with the volume name. To make all volumes available, follow the command with ALL.

multiplexer (MUX) A device that combines signals from several circuits into one signal for more efficient transmission.

multiplexing The use of a single channel or line for several simultaneous trans-

NAK See *negative acknowledgment.*

NAME NetWare v2.2, v3.11 console command to display the file server's name.

name space In NetWare v3.11, memory added to a file server to allow non-DOS files (such as Macintosh files) to be stored on an MS-DOS NetWare volume. The MAC.NAM file, loaded with the LOAD command, allows a DOS file server to be used as a NetWare for Macintosh target file server. The ADD NAME SPACE console command is used to add the memory.

narrowband channel Transmission channel with a speed of 100 to 200 bits per second.

native lock See *lock.*

NBACKUP NetWare BACKUP menu utility that backs up and restores MS-DOS and Macintosh files on file servers and local drives. It is also used to change the current file server attachments. A maximum of eight file servers can be attached, and only attached servers can be backed up or act as backups.

Users with File Scan and Read rights in a directory can back up files in that directory. NetWare v2.x hidden and system directories can be backed up only with NBACKUP v2.2. To use NetWare v3.11 and Portable NetWare BACKUP on hidden and system directories, the directories' attributes must first be changed to make them visible.

Backing up an entire file server requires Supervisory rights.

Restoring information requires the Create, Erase, File Scan, Modify, and Write rights. Files must be restored to the same drive from which they were backed up.

NBIO A driver and module in the IPX/SPX protocol stack.

NBIX A driver and module in the IPX/

SPX protocol stack.

NCC See *NetWare Control Center.*

NCOPY NetWare Network COPY command-line utility used to copy files to another directory. Enter NCOPY, followed by the source path and file, and the target path and file. The filename can be changed as part of the copying procedure.

NCOPY has the following options (entered after the target filename):

- /A (copies only files with an archive bit set, but does not reset the archive bit)
- /M (copies files with archive bit set and also resets the archive bit)
- /Copy (copies files but not their attributes or name space)
- /Subdirectories (copies a directory's subdirectories as well as its files)
- /Empty subdirectories (copies empty subdirectories with /Subdirectories)
- /Force sparse files (forces NetWare to write to sparse files (files containing little data), which it

otherwise would not do)
- /Inform (informs the user when information about attributes or name space cannot be copied)
- /Preserve (copies system and hidden files)
- /Verify (verifies the accuracy of the copying)

NCP Service Protocol See *NetWare Core Protocol.*

NCP A driver and module in the IPX/SPX protocol stack.

NCP engine In Portable NetWare, an NCP process. The maximum number of NCP processes available is set with the NWConfig file, using the max_procs parameter. The number of processes that must exceed the number in use is set with spawn_ahead_procs. The number of clients that can use an NCP engine is set with clients_per_process.

NDIR NetWare Network DIRectory command-line utility that provides information about files and subdirectories. NDIR can manipulate information about a directory's subdirec-

tories and files as a database does, sorting, limiting, and displaying specific information about any of the following: name, file size, date and time created, date and time accessed, files for archiving, date of last archiving, file attributes, file owner, Macintosh files, and subdirectory rights.

NDLIST NetWare Lite command

    net ndlist

that displays the existing network directories.

NE1000 Network board for Ethernet and Ethernet II (Novell), for installation on ISA (AT bus) file servers. The connector type, Remote Reset, base I/O address, and interrupt line must be set, depending on Ethernet type and cabling used.

NE1000.LAN NetWare v3.11 LAN driver that links NetWare to a Novell NE1000 network board installed in a file server. The driver is loaded into the operating system with the following command:

    LOAD NE 1000

The screen may provide prompts for the drive letter or volume name directory path, the driver name and parameter, interrupt, unique I/O port number, frame (packet header), the board's unique name, the node address, and the number of transmission retries after failure.

NE2 Network board for thick or thin Ethernet and Ethernet II (Novell), for installation on Micro Channel (IBM PS/2) file servers for NetWare v2.2 and clients. I/O ports, interrupts, memory addresses, and node addresses are set with the software on the LAN_DRV_109 diskette accompanying the board.

NE2.LAN NetWare v3.11 LAN driver that links NetWare to a Novell NE2 network board installed in a file server. The driver is loaded into the operating system with the following command:

    LOAD LAN NE2

The screen may provide prompts for the drive letter or volume name, directory path, driver name and parameters, the board's slot number, frame (packet header), the board's unique name, the node address, and the

number of transmission retries after failure.

NE2000 Network board for Ethernet and Ethernet II (Novell) for installation on ISA (AT bus) file servers. the timing compatability, configuration option, connector type, and Remote Reset must be set, depending on Ethernet type and cabling used.

NE2000.LAN NetWare v3.11 LAN driver that links NetWare to a Novell NE2000 network board installed on a file server. The driver is loaded into the operating system with the following command:

LOAD NE2000

The screen may provide prompts for driver letter or volume name, directory path, driver name and parameters, frame (packet header), the interrupt number, the board's unique name, the node address, unique I/O port number, and the number of transmission retries after failure.

NE/2-32 Network board for thick or thin Ethernet and Ethernet II (Novell), for installation on 32-bit Micro Channel (IBM PS/2) file servers using NetWare v3.x. The interrupt line, base I/O address, base memory address, and connector type are set from software, usually using the setup or reference program accompanying the computer.

NE232.LAN NetWare v3.11 LAN driver that links NetWare to a NE/2-32 network board (Novell) installed in a file server. The driver is loaded into the operating system with the following command:

LOAD NE232

The screen may provide prompts for the drive letter or volume name, directory path, driver name and parameters, the board's slot number, frame (packet header), the board's unique name, and the number of transmission retries after failure.

NE3200 Network board for thick or thin Ethernet and Ethernet II (Novell), for installation on 32-bit EISA bus computers. The interrupt line and connector type are set from software, usually using the configuration diskette that accompanies the board. The

!NCL07xx.CFG file from the NW386 LAN DRV 3200 diskette should also be added to the configuration diskette.

NE3200.LAN NetWare v3.11 LAN driver that links NetWare to a Novell NE3200 network board installed in a file server. The driver is loaded into the operating system with the following command:

```
LOAD NE3200
```

The screen may provide prompts for the drive letter or volume name, directory path, driver name and parameter, the board's slot number, frame (packet header), the board's unique name, and the number of transmission retries after failure.

negative acknowledge (NAK) In data communications, an error signal sent in reply or acknowledgment of a signal or data from a sender. The ASCII reply is the control character NAK (15 hexadecimal or 21 decimal).

NEMA 5-15.R Three-wire grounded electrical outlet found in offices and houses.

nested A hierarchical arrangement of computer routines called by other routines; a subroutine indented within a routine.

On the Macintosh desktop, a nested folder is one contained in another folder. In NetWare for Macintosh, trustee rights in a folder are inherited by folders nested in it, unless the trustee rights are redefined or covered by a rights mask.

NET$SYS.ERR A NetWare file containing file server error messages, available through the SYSCON utility. In Portable NetWare, error messages can be sent to the file server console by setting the NWConfig file console_flag token to ACTIVE. Setting the token to INACTIVE prevents error messages from being sent to the console. In other versions of NetWare, the errors are automatically sent to the console.

NetBIOS Program for running network operations on MS-DOS computers. Available as an Applications Programming Interface (API).

NetWare provides NetBIOS as an emulation program, NETBIOS.EXE, on the master diskette to be used as part of the boot program. Various parameters can be set, including number of send and receive buffers and number of retries.

In Portable NetWare, the SCONSOLE NetBios *flag* set to AC-TIVE starts NetBIOS with the architecture daemon, as does the NPSConfig file *netbios* token. The *NetBios shim* converts NetBIOS packets to IPX packets. Its name is set in the NPSConfig file with the *net_bios* token. The current name is *nbix*.

NET.CFG NetWare file that contains customized boot procedures not contained in the SHELL.CFG file. It is used, for example, with Open Data-Link Interface (ODI) workstations. It contains information about link support, such as the number of buffers, protocol name, and the name and parameters of the link driver. The file can be created with a text editor.

NET.EXE NetWare Lite file that allows a station to communicate over the network.

NetWare 286 Version of NetWare for 80286 computers. It has been incorporated in and extended with NetWare v2.2.

NetWare 386 Version of NetWare for 80386 computers. It has been incorporated in and extended with NetWare v3.11.

NetWare Control Center (NCC) NetWare for Macintosh utility that sets folder and file attributes, creates user logins, and creates groups. When opened from the Desktop, the NCC opens a file server window. Pull-down menus display and allow altering of volumes, folders and files, users, and groups. The User menu can also be used to create home folders, assign passwords, and assign rights to a user or group.

NetWare Core Protocol (NCP) NetWare communications protocols as defined in the operating system loaded on a file server. The communications between a file server and workstation are governed by procedures contained in the NCP Service Pro-

1) Node 4 wishes to gain a file handle, so it sends an NCP packet containing the code for "give me a file handle".

2) The Kernel receives the NCP packet from Node 4.

3) The Kernel determines that the NCP contains the code for supplying a file handle to the requesting node.

4) The Kernel triggers a set of file system routines that provide the file handle.

5) Node 4 obtains its file handle.

6) The Kernel awaits further NCP packets.

NCPs provide services to NetWare clients by triggering a series of kernel routines.

tocols, which are then formatted according to IPX.

NetWare DA NetWare for Macintosh desk accessory that allows a user with appropriate rights to display or change rights, view or change jobs in the print queue, and communicate with other workstations on the same file server. The NetWare DA is installed in the Apple menu with the Font/DA Mover or a similar application. The NOTIFY Init must also be dragged into the system folder.

NetWare expanded memory shell See *expanded memory shell*.

NetWare extended memory shell See *extended memory shell*.

NetWare for Macintosh Version of NetWare that allows Apple Macintosh computers to run on MS-DOS NetWare networks. NetWare for Macintosh consists of software for the Macintosh Desktop and for the DOS file server.

NetWare for UNIX See *Portable NetWare*.

NetWare Lite Version of NetWare for peer-to-peer networks of two to 25 computers, with one, more than one, or all workstations acting as file servers.

NetWare Loadable Module (NLM) In NetWare v3.11, a utility linked to the operating system that assists and extends network functions. The following NLMS are available: CLIB, DISKSET, EDIT, ETHERRPL, INSTALL, IPXS, MATH-LIB, MATHLIBC, MONITOR, NMAGENT, PSERVER, REMOTE, ROUTE, RS232, RSPX, SPX-CONFG, SPXS, STREAMS TLI, TOKENRPL, UPS, and VREPAIR. All modules are loaded with the LOAD console command.

NLMs that Your Server is Likely to Require for day-to-day operation:

NLM Name	Function
MONITOR.NLM	Displays NetWare's use of server and OS resources.
STREAMS.NLM	Provides NetWare STREAMS environment.
CLIB.NLM	Provides NetWare v3.11 C interface.
REMOTE.NLM	Provides the NetWare v3.11 Remote Console.
RSPX.NLM	Provides a transport service for REMOTE.NLM.
UPS.NLM	Provides UPS monitoring for ther server.
MAC.NAM OS/2.NAM NFS.NAM	Provide name spaces for Macintosh, OS/2 HPFS, and NFS file systems.
NMAGENT.NLM	Collects and monitors server data for use by IBM's NetView network management program.

NetWare Management Agent for NetView Set of NetWare loadable modules for use on a Token-Ring network with a host computer that uses IBM Systems Network Architecture (SNA). NetView is an SNA-related product that allows non-SNA and non-IBM networks to communicate with SNA mainframes. The loadable modules allow a NetWare v3.11 file server's Token-Ring adapter to send NetView Token-Ring LAN alerts and LAN Logical Link Control (LLC) alerts to the host.

NetWare Name Service NetWare global naming or directory service product that allows the network to handle requests for services. It permits creation of a domain of file server and resources, such as printers, so that logging into one server in the domain makes all its servers and resources available. NetWare Name Service consists of a program and utilities that are loaded on top of the NetWare operating system.

network Two or more computers, terminals, printers, and other devices connected by communications lines that permit the exchange of data and the sharing of resources. Communications lines can be twisted-pair (telephone type) wire, coaxial cable, telephone lines connected to computers by modems, and radio wave, satel-

lite, and other wireless methods. Networks can be connected in several designs or topologies, such as bus, linear, star, or ring. Network stations (also called nodes, devices, or workstations) can acquire the line to transmit or receive data by several methods, including polling, token passing, and contention. Some networks are homogeneous systems that use the same type or brand of equipment. Other networks are heterogeneous, or open, systems that use numerous brands of hardware and software. Heterogeneous systems demonstrate *interoperability*.

Networks are often characterized by the geographical area they encompass. A local area network (LAN) usually covers an office, a department, or a building. A metropolitan area network (MAN) covers a wider area, such as a large campus, a town, or a city. A wide area network (WAN) covers a region, a country, or a worldwide area. An internetwork is a network composed of other networks.

Several standard topologies have been defined by professional organizations or commercial firms. The to-

pologies include ARCnet, Ethernet, and Token-Ring. Various software operating systems work with or on top of computer operating systems. For example, NetWare functions as an operating system on top of MS-DOS and as a process under UNIX.

A **logical network** is a path between sending and receiving nodes, regardless of the physical configuration of the network or networks.

network address See *network numbering*.

network analyzer A LAN software tool that monitors communications traffic to detect the causes of faulty packet transmissions and as an aid in improving network efficiency. Such a tool is also called a protocol analyzer.

network board Circuit board installed in a workstation or device that permits the workstation or device to communicate with other network nodes. Boards (also called adapters) are usually specific to a particular network topology, such as Ethernet, and sta-

tion architecture, such as ISA or Micro Channel. Some boards are configured by setting jumpers, others by setting software. Specific types of cabling and adapters are recommended for each board. In NetWare, a network board is linked to the system with a *LAN driver* that has been designed for it.

Frequently, such boards are called **Network Interface Cards** or **NICs**.

network identifier variables In NetWare, variables used with the IF...THEN (v2.2) or IF...THEN...ELSE (v3.11, Portable NetWare) login script command. The variables include conditionals, date, network, time, user, and station variables.

Conditionals include A C C E S S _ S E R V E R , ERROR_LEVEL, and MEMBER OF "group". Date variables include DAY, DAY_OF_WEEK, MONTH, M O N T H _ N A M E , NDAY_OF_WEEK (day number, with Sunday as 1), SHORT_YEAR, and YEAR. Network variables are NETWORK_ADDRESS and FILE_SERVER. Time variables are

AM_PM, GREETING_TIME (morning, afternoon, or evening), HOUR, HOUR24, MINUTE, and SECOND. User variables are FULL_NAME, LOGIN_NAME, and USER_ID. Station variables are MACHINE, OS, OS_VERSION, P_STATION (station number of node address), SHELL_TYPE, SMACHINE, and STATION (connection number).

DOS variables can be used by enclosing them in < > (angle brackets).

network layer Type of function provided for data transmission, usually by means of protocols or specifications. Each layer passes a message between the layers above and below it. A layer at one end of the communications path performs services for incoming and outgoing messages similar to the services performed by the complementary layer at the other end. For example, the ISO/OSI Reference Model contains seven layers: Application, Presentation, Session, Transport, Network, Data-Link, and Physical. NetWare uses a six-layer

model based on the ISO/OSI Reference Model: application, service protocol, communication protocol, link support, driver, and hardware.

network numbering A network's addresses defined in the Transport layer. A set of addresses is also called a set of *sockets*. The address usually includes a number for the network, host, and port; it is defined by a transport protocol. For example, TCP includes a 32-bit network and host address and a 16-bit port address. CCITT includes a four decimal digit network number and a ten digit host and port number.

In NetWare, the address is an eight-digit hexadecimal number (from 1 through FFFFFFFE) including a network number and a node number. In NetWare v3.0 and above, the network address includes an external network number and an internal network number that identifies the logical network. The logical netwo k consists of the path between the send ing and receiving nodes. (See illustration on following page.)

network supervisor See *supervisor, network*.

network topology See *topology*.

network trunk cable A network backbone, composed of all the trunk segments that connect a specific number of nodes over a specific length of cable.

NET*x* NetWare command-line utility that displays the workstation's version of the NetWare shell (option I). Option U unloads the shell. Option PS= allows entry of the name of the file server the workstation will be attached to. It consists of the program NET*x*.COM that loads the NetWare base memory shell as a TSR (terminate-and-stay-resident program) during the system boot process. NET*x* handles communications between the application and MS-DOS, such as calls to DOS functions, error handling, and data being sent to the local printer. NET*x* also assigns sending and receiving addresses to data packets. For instance, it evaluates a request and then passes the request to the local DOS or to IPX/SPX for transfer to the file server. The *x* corresponds

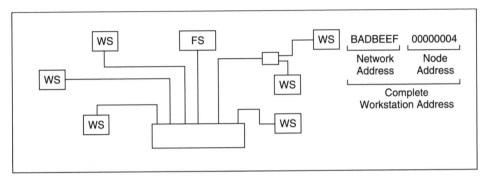

This single network is configured with one network address

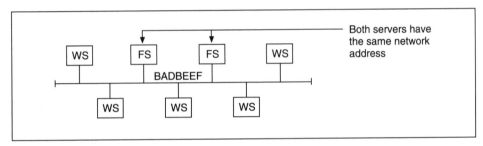

This multiserver network requires the same network address on all its file servers, but a unique node number on each.

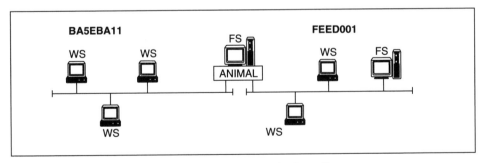

Two networks with different network addresses are brought together in one file server.

to the version of DOS, such as NET4 for DOS version 4.x.

NET$BIND.SYS Hidden file in the NetWare v2.2 SYS:SYSTEM directory that contains objects and properties for the bindery.

NET$BVAL.SYS Hidden file in the NetWare v2.2 SYS:SYSTEM directory that contains property data sets for the bindery.

NET$DOS.SYS NetWare remote boot image file in the file server's SYS:LOGIN directory. It contains a workstation's boot files, which are loaded with the DOSGEN command-line utility. The boot files allow the workstation to be booted from the file server rather than from a boot diskette in the workstation's local disk drive.

NET$OS.EXE NetWare v2.2 file containing the NetWare operating system.

NET$OBJ.SYS NetWare v3.11 file in the SYS:SYSTEM directory that contains the objects for the bindery.

NET$PROP.SYS NetWare v3.11 file in the SYS:SYSTEM directory that contains the properties for the bindery.

NET$VAL.SYS NetWare v3.11 file in the SYS:SYSTEM directory that contains the property data sets for the bindery.

NMAGENT NetWare v3.11 Network Management AGENT loadable module that
must be loaded before LAN drivers are loaded. NMAGENT tracks the drivers and assures that they meet network management requirements. The tracking resources, called Network Management Triggers, Managers, and Objects, can be viewed with the MONITOR loadable module.

node In network communications, a computer, station, terminal, printer, or other device connected to the network. Node also refers to the place where the connection occurs.

node address A node's name or number, used for sending or receiving data. The node name is part of the network's address.

In NetWare, the node address is the node number of a network board. Node addresses can be preset (as on any Ethernet board); set with jumpers or switches (as on the Novell NE1000 board); or set with software (as with the Novell NE2 board. Some boards use a combination of methods.

See also *network numbering*.

node name See *node address*.

node number See *node address*.

noise In signal transmissions, random and unwanted signals from the circuitry or environmental conditions that distort the message signal and may cause data errors.

nondedicated server A workstation that can function as a file server as well as a workstation. For example, when the NetWare Lite SERVER.EXE file is loaded into a workstation's memory, the workstation can function as a nondedicated server.

nonswitched line A line with permanent connections, in contrast to a line that requires dialing to establish the connection. For example, a leased line is a nonswitched line.

nontransparent mode Type of transmission in which control characters can be seen. This mode is used, for example, in binary synchronous communication (BSC or bisync).

no parity See *parity*.

Novell Virtual Terminal (NVT) See *NVT*.

NPLIST NetWare Lite command
```
net nplist
```
that allows a user to see a list of available printers and the user's rights to them.

NPRINT NetWare Network PRINTer command-line utility that allows DOS files or other files to be printed directly on a specific printer rather than from an application. The print job options can be set with NPRINT or with the PRINTCON menu utility.

NPRINT has the following options: NOTIfy (tells the sender that the job has been printed), NoNOTIfy, PrintServer (name), Server (name), Queue (name), Job (configuration), Form, Copies (specifies number of copies to be printed), Tabs, NoTabs, NoBanner, NAMe (specifies name to be included in the banner), Banner (specifies text for the lower part of the banner), NoFormFeed, FormFeed (generates a form feed at the end of the job), and Delete (deletes the file after it has been printed).

NPSConfig Portable NetWare configuration file for the Novell Protocol Suite (NPS), which sets the parameters for network services on the host server. Some of its parameters can be set either within the file or through the SCONSOLE utility.

NPSConfig has the following parameters: *nvt_server_name*, *track_on*, *spx*, *nvt*, *netbios*, *netbios_shim*, *sap*, *nvt_getty_entry*, *nvt_init_level*, *nvt_spawns*, *nvt_line_disc*, *sap_standard_out*, *sap_error_out*, *sap_reply_delay*, *priority*, *capture_lan*, *internal_network*, *lan_1_adapter*, *lan_1_network*, *lan_1_adapter type*, and *lan_1_module*. The *lan_1_packet_type* parameter must be set within the program.

npsd See *architecture daemon.*

null modem A device that allows direct connection of two computers for data communications rather than sending the message over a telephone line.

numbering, device In NetWare, numbers that identify a hard disk. They include the physical address, defined by the disk driver; the device code, which contains information about the disk type, board number, controller number, and disk number; and the logical number, determined by the order in which the drives are loaded.

numbering, network See *network numbering.*

NVER NetWare Network VERsion command-line utility that displays the current versions of NetBIOS, IPX, SPX, LAN driver, shell, and worksta-

tion and file server operating systems.

NVT Portable NetWare Novell Virtual Terminal command-line utility, a device driver loaded as a TSR (ter inate-and-stay-resident program) that allows a station emulating a host terminal to use NetWare to connect directly to the host.

A file server is designated as an NVT server through the NPSConfig file. The *nvt_server_name=* token should contain the server's name between quotation marks (" "). Setting the token *nvt=* ACTIVE instructs the architecture daemon to start NVT. The *NVT Flag* set to ACTIVE allows a station emulating a terminal to communicate with the host. *NVT SERVICE NAME* gives the name of the NVT server. *NVT Gettydefs Entry, NVT Init Level, NVT Spawn Number,* and *NVT Line Discipline* all refer to the pseudo-tty (UNIX communication receiver that looks like a tty file) settings and processes.

These parameters can also be set from the SCONSOLE Edit NVT Parameters screen, via the Configuration Menu and Transport Configuration Menu.

NWConfig Portable NetWare configuration file that sets parameters used by the host system. The following parameters can be set within the file or from the SCONSOLE console command: *spawn_ahead_processes, max_procs, clients_per_process, shm_size, max_connections, max_volumes, file_server_name, binaries, volume, console_device, console_flag, log_watchdog_logouts, display_watchdog_logouts, login, req_password_encryption, shm_key, max_file_size, file_mask, dir_mask, native_locks, read_ahead_cache, read_ahead_cache_block_size, write_behind_flag, alert_notify_list, dir_cache_items, salvage_utility_flag, salvage_num_files,* and *salvage_max_bytes.*

The following parameters can be set only through NWConfig: *config_file_version, stub_volume, language, hu_group_owner, hu_user_owner, print_check_time_delay, shm_access,* and *ipc_access.*

NWENGINES In Portable NetWare, service processes or *NCP engines* used

for logging in and using applications.

object A data structure or data. **Object code** is machine-executable code produced by a compiler or an assembler. An **object module** or **program** is assembled or compiled for execution. An **object file** (MS-DOS extension .OBJ or UNIX extension .o) contains object code. In object-oriented programming, an object contains both data structures and commands or methods for manipulating them.

In the NetWare bindery, an object consists of the names of users, devices, and other physical and logical (design) entities. In NetWare v2.2, bindery objects are contained in the NET$BIND.SYS hidden system file. In NetWare v3.11 and Portable NetWare, the bindery objects are in NET$OBJ.SYS.

odd parity See *parity*.

ODI See *Open Data-Link Interface*.

OFF NetWare v2.2 and v3.11 console command that clears the file server console screen.

Open In NetWare for Macintosh v2.15, an access right that allows a user to open a file or folder. In all other versions of NetWare, the right to open a file, folder, or directory is implied in the Create, Read, and Write rights.

Open Data-Link Interface (ODI) NetWare software for use in open systems. ODI allows one network board, LAN driver, and cabling system to emulate various communications hardware and protocols, such as AppleTalk, IPX/SPX, and TCP/IP, and to use them interchangeably.

ODI supports Ethernet, Ethernet-II, Token-Ring, ARCnet, and IBM PC network frames and LAN drivers.

A workstation whose AUTOEXEC.BAT file contains the ODI LSL.COM file (providing the NetWare Link Support Layer) can communicate with a NetWare file

139

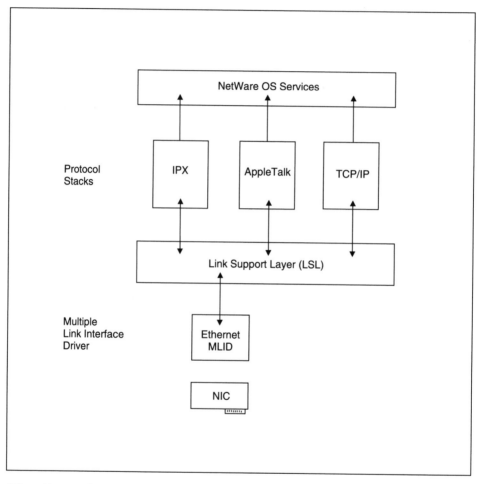

ODI provides a standard interface for allowing transport protocols to share a single network card without conflict.

server. The file should also contain the LAN driver, protocol stacks, and NetWare shell. See illustration left.

open system Computer system composed of many different brands of computers, buses, cables, printers, and other devices and software linked by common standards and protocols. An example is NetWare Open Data-Link Interface (ODI).

operation A computer action that carries out a command or instruction. In network communications, a transmission mode such as synchronous or asynchronous, or full- or half-duplex.

orphaned packets In data transmission, packets in a numbered sequence that are dropped because one packet was received out of order. A count of orphaned packets is a feature of the TRXNET LAN driver used with RX-Net boards in ARCnet networks.

OSI See *ISO/OSI*.

overlay file NetWare files (with the .OVL extension) that are used in tailoring

screen displays to the monitor type and to the user's taste. The IBM$RUN.OVL file is used for IBM color monitors and windowing; the CMPQ$RUN.OVL file is used for non-IBM monochrome monitors.

packet A message block containing data. The packet also contains addressing, control, and error detection information for transmission. The size and components of a packet depend on the communications protocol being used. Some protocols send packets in sequence. Other protocols send the packets in random order; the packets are correctly assembled at the receiving node.

In NetWare, a packet header's transmission request information is supplied by the NetWare Core Protocol (NCP), the packet length and sender information by IPX, and the physical address by the device driver. (See illustration on following page.)

packet assembler/disassembler (PAD) Software that divides data into packets for transmission and reassembles incoming packets.

packet receive buffer In NetWare v3.11, file server memory area for temporary storage of incoming data packets until they are sent to their receiving nodes.

In v2.2, this memory area is called a *communication buffer*.

packet-switched data network (PSDN) A *packet-switching* communications network (wide area network) that uses the CCITT *X.25* standard.

packet switching Packet transmission over channels that are dedicated only during the actual transmission. When the transmission is completed, the channel is released for other uses. A network that uses this procedure is called a **packet-switched data network** (PSDN).

PAD See *packet assembler/disassembler; padding*.

padding Adding of characters, such as nulls or zeros, to data to fill up a fixed-length field or other structure. Removing such characters is called *unpadding*.

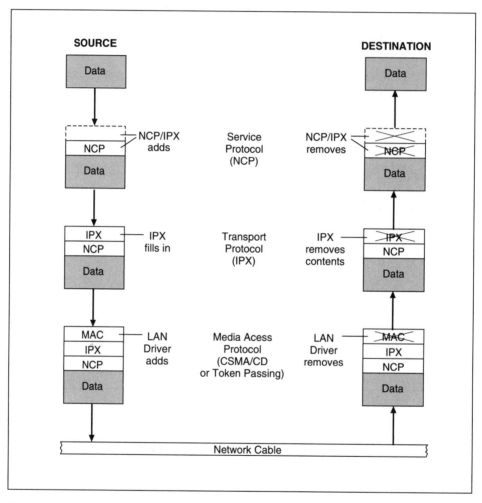

When a packet is sent, each communication layer adds its own header information, which is removed in reverse order at the destination.

In Portable NetWare, **PAD** is a token for the NPSConfig *lan_1_module* file parameter that increases the length of Ethernet packets beyond the minimum. The **PAD_AND_ADD_SAP** token increases the length of Ethernet packets to the minimum length.

palette See *color palette.*

parallel transmission The transfer of data more than one bit at a time. A **parallel input/output port** supports parallel transmission, often from a computer to a printer (usually referred to as a **parallel printer**). On IBM and compatible computers, parallel ports are called LPT1, LPT2, and LPT3.
A **parallel interface** is hardware that connects devices using parallel transmission.

parent In hierarchical data structures and programming, such as data trees and object-oriented programming, a node or object that has descendants below it in the hierarchy. The parent passes its characteristics on to its descendants.

In UNIX, a **parent process** is an existing process that is replicated with the call *fork*, forming a *child process.*

In the NetWare volume hierarchy, a parent is a volume or directory that has a directory, subdirectory, or file as a descendant. The term is used, for example, in the Restore Options screen of the NetWare v3.11 SBACKUP loadable module; this screen is displayed when data is being restored to a file server.

Parental Access right in NetWare for Macintosh v2.15. In other versions of NetWare, this right is called Access Control.

parity In data communications, a method of checking errors involving the number of binary ones in a set of bits. An extra bit (called a **parity bit**) is added that makes the number of ones transmitted either even (**even parity**) or odd (**odd parity**). A parity error in data received indicates a transmission error.

Horizontal parity is applied by bytes; **vertical parity** is applied to the same bit position in a group of bytes.

The method is also called **parity checking** or *redundancy checking*.

partition, hard disk The division of hard disk storage space for a particular use, such as for a specific operating system. In NetWare, an internal disk drive can be partitioned into DOS and NetWare sections. External drives are used only for NetWare.

In NetWare v2.2, a disk is partitioned with the INSTALL program's File Server Definition Screen, available after disks have been prepared for NetWare. Selecting Non-bootable from the Partition Status menu allows the user to make space for another operating system by changing the size of End Cylinder or Megabytes.

In NetWare v3.11, disk partitions are created with the INSTALL loadable module's Create Partition command in the Partition Options Menu, via the Installation Options Menu, Disk Options Menu, Available Disk Options Menu, and Partition Tables. Partition size and Hot Fix information are added by the network supervisor.

Mirroring or *duplexing* can also be done at this time.

In Portable NetWare, a portion of the host computer's disk is set aside for the NetWare operating system. (See illustration on following page.)

passive hub See *hub*.

password A word or set of alphanumeric characters allowing access to a facility, computer, or network. In network security, a password is a character string that verifies a user's identity and permits access to the system. The password may be accompanied by some other unique identifier before the user is allowed to log in.

NetWare allows passwords in login scripts, in which case each user must have a password. The network supervisor determines whether each user's password must be unique (different from the ten preceding passwords used by the account). Using the SYSCON menu utility, passwords can be assigned, limited, and changed through system defaults or through each user's login script and account.

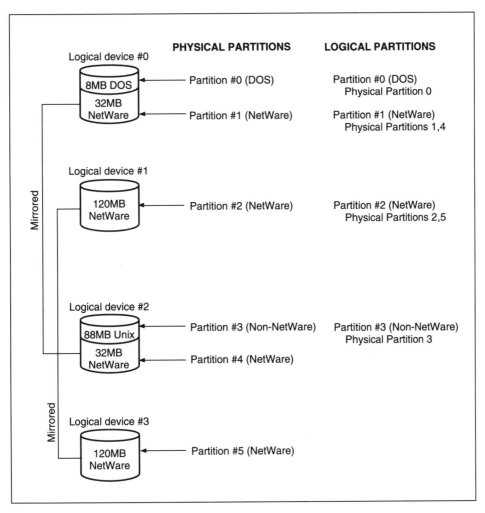

Internal disk drives partitioned into DOS and NetWare sections.

Passwords can be set or changed with the SETPASS command-line utility.

If users are permitted to change their own passwords, they must have access rights to edit their own login scripts.

Passwords are required for remote setup, and are specified with the RSETUP menu utility.

In NetWare v3.x and above, passwords can be encrypted for decoding by the file server. Passwords are encrypted with the SET console command *Allow Unencrypted Passwords* = parameter. The default is OFF. The parameter must also be changed in the AUTOEXEC.NCF file, through INSTALL or SYSCON, with the following command:

```
SET ALLOW UNENCRYPTED
PASSWORDS =
```

The command should include the setting ("on" or "off").

PASSWORD_EXPIRES In NetWare v2.2 a login script command used with an IF...THEN statement to alert a user to the amount of time left before the password can no longer be used.

patch cable See *cable*.

path In hierarchical data structures, such as operating system directories, the chain from a root directory (as in MS-DOS) or volume (NetWare) to a specific subdirectory or file.

In data communications, the transmission route from sending node to receiving node, making up a *logical network*.

PAUDIT NetWare Print AUDIT command-line utility in the SYS:SYSTEM directory that displays in chronological order the system's accounting records contained in the NET$ACCT.DAT file.

This information can be redirected or piped to a DOS file with the following command:

```
PAUDIT >filename
```

The information can also be saved or it can be printed with the NPRINT command-line utility.

PAUSE NetWare login script command that stops execution of the script and displays the following message:

```
Strike a key when ready...
```

Execution resumes after any key is pressed.

The word WAIT can be used instead of PAUSE.

PCCOMPATIBLE NetWare login script command that must be included if the workstation is IBM-compatible, but the long machine name in the workstation's SHELL.CFG file reads otherwise. The command can also be written as:

```
COMPATIBLE
```

PCN2 Network board for installation in IBM PS/2 workstations.

PCN2.LAN NetWare LAN driver that links NetWare to a PCN2 network board (IBM) installed in an IBM PS/2 workstation. The driver is loaded into the operating system with the following command:

```
LOAD LAN PCN2
```

The command must include the drive letter or volume name and directory path and the driver name and parameters. The unique I/O port number is a required parameter. Frame (packet header), the board's unique name,

and the node address are optional parameters. The user will be prompted for parameters not included in the command line.

PCN2RPL NetWare v3.11 loadable module containing the protocol stack for remotely booting IBM PS/2 workstations that have PCN2 network boards installed.

PCONSOLE NetWare Print CONSOLE menu utility used to make or dissolve other file server attachments and provide print queue and print server information. The Change Current File Server option (selected from the Available Options Menu) allows the user to attach to additional file servers, withdraw from any file server but the default, select a file server to be the current file server in order to make printing arrangements, and change to the name of the new current file server's user.

The Print Queue Information menu option allows the user to print a file by defining the job and sending it to the queue. The option also allows the user to create, delete, or rename

queues and assign or remove queue operators and users. The user can change operator flags, such as allowing users to place jobs in the print queue, allowing the print server to service queue jobs, and allowing additional print servers to attach to the queue. It also provides print server and print job information.

The Print Server Information menu option allows the user to change the printer configuration, including the name, whether the printer is parallel or serial, whether the printer is local or remote, the interrupt signal value, buffer size, and type of paper (form) to be used. The baud, number of data and stop bits, parity, and use of X-ON/X-OFF can also be selected for serial printers. The option also allows the user to create, delete, and rename print servers, select the print server password, attach file servers to a print server, and take a print server down. It also provides print server information. In addition, the option allows printers to be added to and removed from the print server.

PDF See *printer definition files*.

peer-to-peer Data communication or data processing that moves from one processor to another, such as between workstations or between workstation and mainframe. The term is also used for *program-to-program*, as in IBM's Advanced Program-to-Program Communications (APPC) Session layer protocol.

permission See *grant*.

phase modulation (PM) Method of transmitting an information signal by changing (modulating) the phase of the carrier wave.

phaser See *FIRE PHASERS*.

physical Actual computers, workstations, processors, cabling, software and other equipment used in a communications network, based on its *logical* design. A **physical address** is the actual address of a node or of memory, contrasted with the logical or virtual address in a program.

Physical layer Layer 1 of the ISO/OSI Reference Model for open system

networking. This layer carries the unformatted incoming and outgoing data.

physical lock See *lock*.

physical network See *topology*.

physical topology See *topology*.

plain folder See *security*.

PID See *protocol identification number*.

PIN number Personal identification number, a unique identifier that allows user access to a computer network. An example is the number users enter in an automatic teller machine or for electronic transfer of funds.

piping The use of the output of one command as the input of another, a feature of MS-DOS and UNIX. A NetWare example is the redirection or piping of data from the PAUDIT command-line utility to a DOS file for saving or printing. The DOS symbol is > or l.

A **pipeline** is the output command and the input command. In UNIX, the two are linked by the l operator .

PNWSTATUS Portable NetWare STATUS command-line utility that displays on a host terminal screen whether Portable NetWare is running on the host.

point-to-point Communication circuit between two nodes in which the message transmitted from one node is received in its entirety by the second node. If the path includes several intermediate nodes, each of which receives the entire message before passing it on, it is called *store-and-forward*.

A **point-to-point link**, as defined by the IEEE, is a link segment with an end-to-end propagation delay of no more than 2,570 ns.

poll Method of determining when a network node can transmit. The network controller requests nodes' status at specified intervals. A node can transmit only when it is polled by the controller. An example in NetWare is a printing process polling a print queue for jobs.

port In data communications, a hardware device that connects a computer with a printer or other peripheral device. It is often called an *input/output port* or an *I/O port*.

Portable NetWare Version of NetWare for use with UNIX and other non-DOS operating systems. In UNIX systems, the Portable NetWare file server runs as a set of processes on the host computer, rather than on a dedicated file server.

Presentation layer Layer 6 of the ISO/OSI Reference Model for open system networking. This layer translates messages between the network software's format and an international standard format used for transmission.

PRINT NetWare Lite command, net print, followed by the path and filename, and used to print a file. To send the file to a network printer, the port must be captured with the following command:

```
net capture
```

Follow the filename with the name of a specified network printer and necessary flags.

PRINTCON NetWare PRINT job CONfiguration menu utility used to edit, select, and copy print job configurations. Each user can create and change configurations in a PRINTCON.DAT file stored in the MAIL ID directory. These configurations are used with the CAPTURE, NPRINT, and PCONSOLE utilities.

Selecting Edit Print Job Configurations from the PRINTCON Available Options Menu permits the user to create, edit, rename, and delete configurations, select the default configuration, and copy another user's configuration.

A print job configuration created in PRINTCON can specify the following parameters:
- Number of copies to be printed
- Whether the file is text (ASCII text) or byte stream (formatted and printed from within an application)
- Tab spaces (for an ASCII text file)
- Form feed
- Notification that the print job is completed
- Form (type of paper) used
- Whether a banner will be printed
- Name at the top of the banner

- Banner name (text at the bottom of the banner)
- Whether a local parallel printer port is to be captured
- Whether auto endcap is to be used
- Enable timeout (when a job will be sent to the print queue with capture or ENDCAP)
- Timeout count (the elapsed time before data goes to the print queue)
- File server name
- Print queue name
- Print server name
- Device name (printer or plotter)
- Printing mode

PRINTDEF NetWare PRINTer DEFinition menu utility that is used to create printer, plotter, and form (paper) definitions to be used with PRINTCON. Definitions for numerous widely used printing devices are supplied as .PDF files with NetWare and stored in the SYS:PUBLIC directory. A user can import the .PDF files into PRINTDEF. Definitions can also be written or copied from another file server.

PRINTER NetWare v2.2 core printing console command for controlling print jobs for networks not using NetWare Name Service. The PRINTER, or P, command used without options lists information about printers attached to the file server. The PRINTER command can include the following options: ADD QUEUE (add the name of an already-created queue), CONFIG (display the printer configuration), CREATE (modify a serial printer configuration), DELETE QUEUE, FORM FEED, FORM MARK (mark the top of form), HELP, MOUNT FORM (change paper type), POLL (specify the amount of elapsed time before a print queue is polled for print jobs), QUEUE (list the queues and their priorities), REWIND (rewind the printer a specified number of pages), START (restart a printer after a stop command), and STOP (stop a print job).

printer definition (.PDF) files NetWare .PDF files containing definitions for printers. Some files are provided with NetWare and are placed in SYS:PUBLIC during operating system installation. Definitions can also

be written or imported from other file servers.

print server Network computer that handles printing needs of workstations. It can be dedicated or nondedicated.

NetWare print services can use either a dedicated print server with a printer attached or a workstation acting as a nondedicated print server with its printer. A dedicated print server uses the PSERVER.EXE executable file, which is loaded during installation or from the DOS prompt and placed in the SYS:PUBLIC directory.

A nondedicated print server uses the PSERVER.VAP (v2.2) value added process, which runs on a file server or external bridge/router. In v3.11, the configuration is dedicated.

In Portable NetWare, print jobs are sent from a file server queue to host print services and printers.

print server operator In NetWare, a person with supervisor rights for managing the print server.

printer queue See *queue.*

Private NetWare v2.2 directory attribute that prevents users from seeing subdirectories unless they have the File Scan right. Private is set with the FLAGDIR command-line utility, whose use requires the Modify right.

In NetWare for Macintosh, the Private attribute is displayed on the Desktop as a gray folder.

privileges See *access privileges; access rights.*

process In UNIX terminology, one execution of a program by one user. Processes are catalogued in a process table. The Portable NetWare file server runs as a set of processes, also referred to as engines, on the host computer. The SCONSOLE utility lets the network supervisor use the *spawn_ahead_procs* token to specify the number of NCP engines (NWENGINES) spawned (created) ahead of those already in use.

program-to-program See *peer-to-peer.*

PP P P

property In NetWare, a characteristic or feature of a bindery object, such as a user's address, password, or account. In v2.2, bindery properties are contained in the NET$BIND.SYS hidden file. In v3.11 and Portable NetWare, they are in NET$PROP.SYS.

protected mode router See *router*.

protocol A set of rules or specifications used to perform a task. In data communications, protocols determine the format and timing of data transfers. Network protocols determine the length of data units and the network requirements. Protocols also establish transmission paths, and provide error checking and addressing. The most comprehensive model for communications protocols is the ISO/OSI Reference Model, which has been the basis for many widely used protocol sets, such as TCP/IP, NetBIOS, and AppleTalk.

NetWare protocols are grouped under IPX/SPX and require specific network boards. Novell's Open Data-Link Interface (ODI) software for open systems allows one board to emulate

boards for various other protocols.

PROTOCOL NetWare v3.11 console command that displays the protocols registered on a file server, together with the names of their frame types and protocol identification numbers as included by the LAN driver when it is installed.

The **PROTOCOL REGISTER** command allows other protocols to be added. After the PROTOCOL or PROTOCOL REGISTER command, enter the name of a protocol, the frame type, and the protocol identification number.

After a protocol has been added, use the BIND console command to bind the protocol to the LAN driver.

protocol analyzer See *network analyzer*.

protocol identification number (PID) Hexadecimal number that identifies the communication protocol used by a board. Other names for protocol identification number are *SAP* or, for Ethernet, *type* or *E-type*.

PSC NetWare command-line utility used

by print server operators for print server and printer control. Most of the PSC commands can also be performed through PCONSOLE. Follow PSC with *PS=* (print server) or *P=* (printer) and any of the following configuration options: ABort (abort the print job), CancelDown (cancel the DOWN command that was issued with PCONSOLE), FormFeed, Keep (place the job at the top of the queue again), Mark (mark the page line where printing will begin), MOunt form (use a new type of paper), PAUse, PRIvate (have exclusive use of a printer), SHAred (remove the PRIvate option), STARt, STATus, and STOp (stop printing).

A network user can use STATus.

PSDN See *packet-switched data network.*

PSERVER NetWare file that provides print services to a network. A dedicated print server uses the PSERVER.EXE executable file, which is loaded during installation or from the DOS prompt and placed in the SYS:PUBLIC directory. A nondedicated print server uses either the PSERVER.VAP (v2.2) value added process, which runs on a file server or external bridge/router, or the PSERVER.NLM (v3.11) loadable module, which is loaded into the file server. (See illustrations on following page.)

pseudo tty UNIX communication receiver that a program treats like a tty file. In Portable NetWare, the NetWare Virtual Terminal (NVT) command-line utility contains several tokens that refer to the pseudo tty used by clients running terminal emulation software: *nvt_getty_entry* defines the I/O setting; *nvt_init_level* and *nvt_spawns* set the run level and number of pseudo tty processes to be spawned; *nvt_line_disc* refers to the line discipline driver.

PSTAT NetWare v2.2 command-line utility that shows on the screen whether a specified printer is online or active.

PS110 board See *RX-Net/2 board.*

PUBLIC NetWare directory that contains files in general use, such as utilities

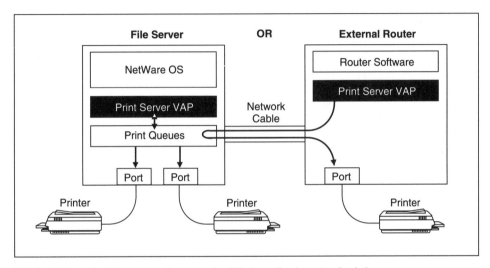

With the VAP-based print server, you have more flexibility in configuring network printing.

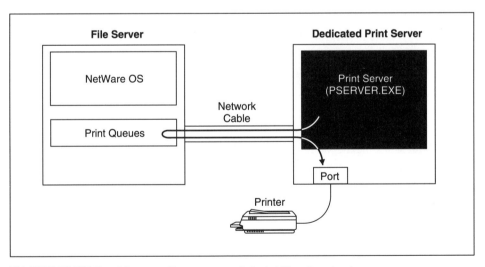

With PSERVER.EXE, the print server software runs on a dedicated PC on the network.

and overlay and other files used for running menu utilities. A user's login script contains a mapping to PUBLIC, and File Scan and Read rights are assigned to each user. PUBLIC is automatically created in the SYS volume when the network is installed.

Files available to all users, called **public files**, are placed in PUBLIC.

public key encryption See *encryption*.

Purge NetWare directory or file attribute that prevents a file from being salvaged after it has been deleted.

PURGE NetWare command or utility that makes deleted files unsalvageable. In NetWare v2.2, PURGE is available as a command-line utility or a console command.

In NetWare v3.11 and Portable NetWare, PURGE is a command-line utility that makes deleted files unsalvageable in the current directory. To purge files in both the current directory and its subdirectories, use the following command:

```
PURGE /ALL
```
Groups of files can also be purged,

as can files owned by the user that are on other NetWare v3.x file servers (but not on v2.x file servers). The SALVAGE utility can also be used to purge files.

NETWARE DECODER

query Request from a database for instructions, status, data, or other information. A query includes limits on the information and the criteria required to find and display the information.

queue A series of messages waiting to be transmitted in the order in which they were received. An example is a series of print jobs waiting to be printed.

In NetWare, each print queue is created with the PCONSOLE menu utility and has its own directory, in which print jobs are stored. Print queues are assigned to defined printers, allowing the print server to properly direct the print job.

The network supervisor is the print queue operator and all network users (in the group EVERYONE) have rights. These initial assignments can be changed. Priorities in the queue, normally first in, first out, can also be changed. See illustration next page.

QUEUE NetWare V2.2 console command used with non-NNS (NetWare Name Service) networks to manipulate queues and print jobs in a queue. The command alone lists print queue information, including name, number of jobs, and number of printers available to the queue. Options include HELP (summarizes QUEUE commands), CHANGE JOB to PRIORITY (priority 1 moves a job to the head of the queue), CREATE (creates a new queue), DELETE JOB, DESTROY (deletes the queue), and JOBS (provides information about the jobs in a queue).

NNS networks use PCONSOLE instead of QUEUE.

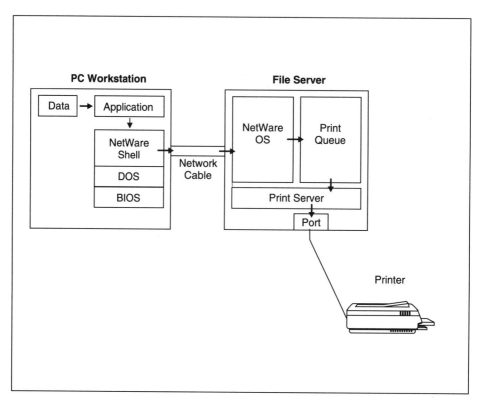

Print jobs redirected to queues on the file server.

raw transmission NetWare's Ethernet transmission packet, consisting of the IEEE 802.3 frame without an 802.2 header. The so-called 802.3 raw frame uses an IPX/SPX header.

RCONSOLE
NetWare v3.11 and Portable NetWare Remote CONSOLE menu utility that allows a workstation to be used as a virtual file server console. After a network supervisor enters RCONSOLE, the screen displays a list of eligible file servers — those with the REMOTE module (which makes the file server console available) and the RSPX module (the SPX driver) already loaded. One server can be selected at a time. File server tasks that can be performed remotely include issuing console commands, copying files to either the NetWare or DOS directories, rebooting the file server, and adding LAN drivers or disk drivers. (See illustration on following page.)

Read NetWare directory right that permits a user to open and read its files. In v3.11, the right can also be granted for individual files (386 only).

Read Audit Security file attribute (Ra) provided for, but not used by NetWare.

Read Only NetWare security attribute (Ro) that allows a file to be opened and read, but not modified. A file has either this attribute or Read Write (Rw). Read Only can be changed by a user who has been granted the Modify right in the file.

When this attribute is assigned in NetWare v3.11 and Portable NetWare, the Delete Inhibit and Rename Inhibit attributes are also assigned.

Read Write NetWare security file attribute (Rw) that allows a file to be read and modified. Removing the attribute automatically adds the Read Only (Ro) attribute. When Read Write is assigned in NetWare v3.11 and Portable

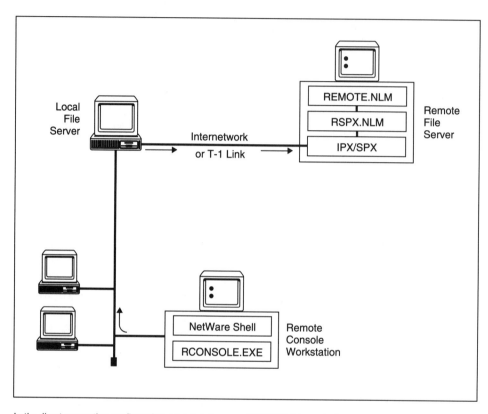

In the direct connection configuration, a workstation uses RCONSOLE to control a remote server.

NetWare, the Delete Inhibit and Rename Inhibit attributes cannot be assigned.

real mode router See *router*.

receive In network communications, to be the final or intermediate addressee of an incoming message. For example, a computer, a printer, or a router can be a receiver.

RECEIVE NetWare Lite command (net receive on) for receiving messages at a workstation, or for preventing messages from being received (net receive off).

record A grouping of associated data fields in a database file. A record is also called a row.

recovery, data See *salvage*.

Red Book U.S. Department of Defense and National Security Agency security policies for networks, so-called from the color of its cover. The Red Book and the Orange Book (for individual systems) are collectively referred to as the "Jell-O Books."

redundancy checking See *parity*.

REGISTER MEMORY NetWare v3.11 console command that allows the operating system to address memory above 16MB in ISA (AT bus) computers. The additional memory can be displayed with the MONITOR loadable module. To see how much memory the operating system is currently addressing, use the MEMORY console command.

rem or **remark** A nonexecutable statement in a computer program, entered as documentation or as a reminder to the programmer. In a NetWare login script, **REMARK**, **rem**, * , or ; at the beginning of a line indicates that what follows is not to be executed.

REMIRROR NetWare v2.2 console command that reactivates mirroring or duplexing on a hard disk after a mirrored or duplexed hard disk either has been unmirrored or has failed and been repaired or replaced.

remote In computer networks, descriptive of a device connected to a controller by a data link, such as a cable or telephone line, rather than by a direct connection. A **remote station** or **remote terminal** is a station or terminal connected to a network by a bridge or router. (See illustration next page.)

In NetWare, a **remote console** (v3.11, Portable NetWare) is a workstation that becomes a virtual file server console through the RCONSOLE menu utility. For a file server to be controlled remotely, it must have the REMOTE module (which makes the file server console available) and the RSPX module (the SPX driver) loaded. Using a remote console to perform file server tasks is called *remote management*.

NET$DOS.SYS is a **remote boot image file** that contains a workstation's boot files. It is loaded into a file server with the DOSGEN command-line utility, permitting the workstation to be booted from the file server rather than from a boot diskette in a local drive.

REMOTE NetWare (v3.11, Portable NetWare) loadable module that allows a file server to be controlled from a workstation functioning as a remote console. The RSPX module must be loaded into the file server after REMOTE is loaded or REMOTE will not function properly.

remote console operator See *remote management*.

remote initial program load (RIPL) NetWare routine installed with Requester that allows remote booting of a diskless workstation.

remote management Use of a remote console by either a network supervisor or a *remote console operator* (a user designated by the network supervisor) to perform file server tasks. Tasks include issuing console commands, copying files to either the NetWare or DOS directories, rebooting the file server, installing NetWare, and adding LAN drivers or disk drivers. However, users cannot be created nor rights assigned remotely.

remote procedure calls NetWare devel-

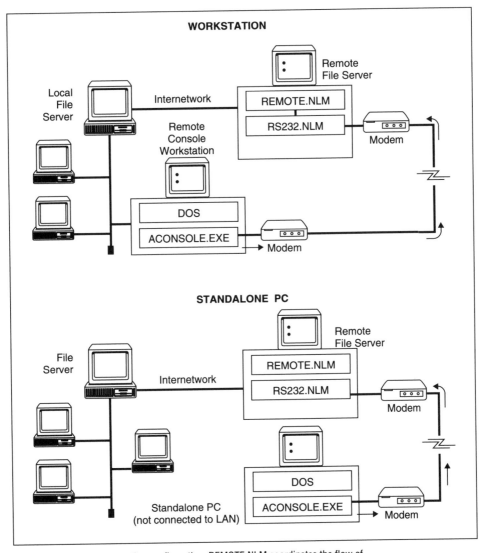

In this asynchronous connection configuration, REMOTE.NLM coordinates the flow of keyboard and monitor information to and from the RS232.NLM driver. As always, it also handles the remote access to the server's keyboard, screen, and file system.

oper tools for client/server applications.

remote reset See *remote*.

remove In NetWare, the process of completely removing a user or group as a trustee of a directory, subdirectory, or file. This can be done with the REMOVE command-line utility, the MAKEUSER menu utility, or the SYSCON menu utility.

Removing a trustee differs from revoking some or all of a trustee's rights, in which case the user or group remains a trustee.

REMOVE NetWare command-line utility used to remove a user or group as a directory trustee. Follow REMOVE with the user's or group's name. To avoid ambiguous names, precede the name with either USER or GROUP. The name can be followed with FROM and a complete path designation. To remove the name from all path subdirectories in NetWare v2.2, add the /SUB option. To remove a name from a subdirectory in NetWare v3.11 and Portable NetWare, follow the user's name with FROM and the path or mapped drive. To remove the name from a file, add the filename.

REMOVE DOS NetWare v3.11 console command that removes DOS from a file server's memory. It prevents loading of modules from DOS drives or the hard disk's DOS partition, makes the memory available to the disk cache, allows warm rebooting of the file server from EXIT, and allows remote rebooting under RCONSOLE.

Rename Inhibit NetWare (v3.11, Portable NetWare) security attribute (R) that prevents the name of a file or directory from being changed, unless a user with the Modify right first removes this attribute. Rename Inhibit is automatically assigned to a file when the Read Only attribute is assigned.

RENDIR NetWare REName DIRectory command-line utility that allows a user with Modify rights in a directory to change the directory's name or the

names of its subdirectories without changing any of the characteristics, such as users' rights. Login script mappings must be modified to reflect any name change.

Requester NetWare program (on the REQUESTER diskette) that allows a workstation running under OS/2 to communicate through a NetWare network by attaching to a file server. Installation of Requester involves specifying the hard disk directories where the Requester files will be stored, editing the CONFIG.SYS file to specify the network board's LAN driver and printing options, and copying the program files. See illustration next page.

repeater Network device that connects two similar trunk segments, receiving a signal that may have been degraded over distance, strengthening it or restoring its original shape, and sending it to the next segment. A repeater permits a LAN or other network to be enlarged by allowing signals to travel longer distances.

RESET ROUTER NetWare (v2.2, v3.11) console command that immediately rebuilds a functioning file server or router's *routing table*. RESET ROUTER initiates a special router request for information, rather than waiting for the next automatic table updating.

resistor Insulated metallic or carbon-based substance that resists electrical current flow. A resistor is used, for instance, as a computer ground to dissipate static electricity.

resource Widely used term for a computer or network device or facility involved in processing data. In NetWare, it means a network board, network device, or other feature using interrupt lines, direct memory access (DMA) lines, input/output addresses, and memory addresses.

response time In data communications, the time between the generation of a message's last character and the receipt of the reply's first character.

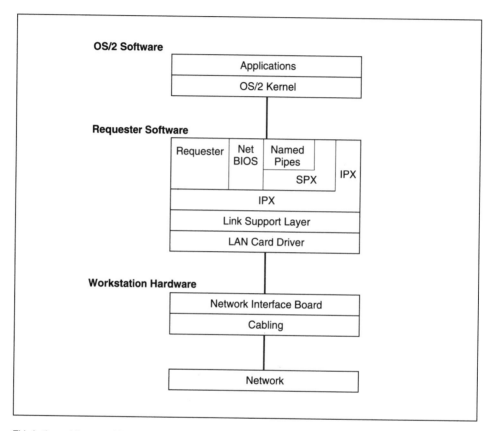

This is the architecture of NetWare Requester.

restore To bring back something that is lost, such as computer data or files that have been lost through tampering or other corruption or a hardware malfunction. To protect against such loss, back up files frequently. If files are lost, they can be restored from the most recent backup copy after the cause has been determined and solved.

In NetWare v2.2 and v3.11, MS-DOS and Macintosh files can be backed up and restored with the NBACKUP menu utility. Restoring information requires the Create, Erase, File Scan, Modify, and Write rights. In Portable NetWare, restoration is performed with the SCONSOLE Backup/Restore Menu.

In NetWare v3.11, the SBACKUP module can be used to restore files at the server backed up on tape with a storage device.

The NetWare Transaction Tracking System (TTS) also restores database data by providing *rollback* in the case of failed transactions.

retransmission Resending a message when the previous transmission has been unsuccessful because of error, lack of an acknowledgment, or a negative acknowledgement.

reverse channel During a message transmission, a separate channel on which the receiver sends an error control, network diagnostic, or other nondata signal to the sender. This channel is also called a *backward channel*.

reverse interrupt In binary synchronous communication, a DLE (data link escape) signal from the receiver in place of an acknowledgment, requesting termination of the transmission before it is completed. In ASCII, DLE is 10 hexadecimal or 16 decimal.

revoke In data communications security systems, the withdrawal by an administrator of a user's previously granted permission to use data.

In NetWare, rights can be revoked with the REVOKE command-line utility or the SYSCON menu utility. The process of revoking rights does not remove the user or group as a trustee.

REVOKE NetWare command-line utility used to revoke a user's or group's specified rights in a directory or file. Follow REVOKE with the abbreviation of the right or rights being revoked: ALL, Access Control, Create, File Scan, Erase, Modify, Read, Supervisory (v3.11), or Write.

In NetWare v2.2, add the /SUB option to revoke a user's or group's specified rights to all path subdirectories. To revoke rights to a subdirectory in NetWare v3.11 and Portable NetWare, follow the rights with FOR and the path or drive mapping, if necessary. Then type FROM and the user's or group's name. To revoke the rights to a file, insert the filename after FOR.

RG58A/U Coaxial cable, 0.2 in., 50 ohm, used for thin Ethernet.

RG-58
50 ohm
cable

right In data and network security, the granting of access to all or part of a system for specified purposes. Rights can also be withheld or revoked. A synonym for right is *privilege*.

NetWare and NetWare for Macintosh v2.2 permit the following rights: Access Control, Create, Erase, File Scan, Erase, Modify, Read, and Write. NetWare v3.11, NetWare for Macintosh v3.*x*, and Portable NetWare permit the same rights and also the Supervisor right. The right to open a file is implied in the other rights.

In NetWare for Macintosh v2.15, the Access Control right is called Parental, Erase is called Delete, and File Scan is called Search. That version also has an Open right.

The rights to a NetWare network take several forms. One or more rights or no rights may be granted to a user or a group for access to a directory and its file or , in v3.11, to a specific file. These are called *trustee right* s (3.x only). In addition, the same rights cover a directory or a file through the Maximum Rights Mask (v2.2) or Inherited Rights Mask (v3.11, Portable NetWare).

A user's *effective rights* for any file or directory are a combination of

the already granted trustee rights, those granted any group the user is part of, and the file or directory rights that are active (have not been revoked) through the mask. A user can view his or her effective rights with the RIGHTS command-line utility, the FILER menu utility, or the WHOAMI command-line utility.

In addition, files have *attributes* that also protect them and take precedence over all rights. (See illustration on following page.)

RIGHTS NetWare command-line utility that displays a list of a user's *effective rights* in a file or a directory. Enter the command, followed by a path or drive mapping, if necessary.

ring network Logical topology of a network in which nodes are connected in a circular pattern, without a hub or central station. An example is the Token-Ring network.

See also *topology*.

RIPL See *remote initial program load*.

RJ11 Standard jack used in homes and offices for telephone and modem wall connections.

RJ45 Jack used for data lines, such as twisted-pair Ethernet cabling.

rollback Negation of file or system changes made in the course of a transaction that is not completed, either because of problems and errors or by user preference. A rollback returns data to the condition it was in before the transaction was initiated. This process is also called *backing out.*

The NetWare Transaction Tracking System (TTS) performs rollback for database operations. It copies existing data before it is overwritten by the current transaction. If the current transaction fails, the backout restores the copied data.

ROUTE NetWare v2.2 value added process (VAP) and v3.11 loadable module (NLM) that determines and monitors a frame's routing over an IBM Token-Ring network. ROUTE is used with the TOKEN LAN driver to send NetWare packets over an IBM Token-Ring network with two types

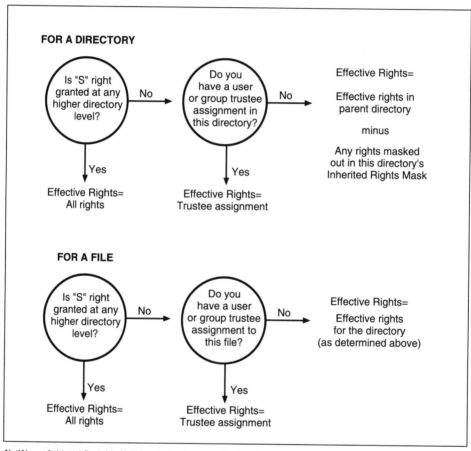

FOR A DIRECTORY

Is "S" right granted at any higher directory level?

No → Do you have a user or group trustee assignment in this directory?

No → Effective Rights= Effective rights in parent directory

minus

Any rights masked out in this directory's Inherited Rights Mask

Yes ↓ Effective Rights= All rights

Yes ↓ Effective Rights= Trustee assignment

FOR A FILE

Is "S" right granted at any higher directory level?

No → Do you have a user or group trustee assignment to this file?

No → Effective Rights= Effective rights for the directory (as determined above)

Yes ↓ Effective Rights= All rights

Yes ↓ Effective Rights= Trustee assignment

NetWare v3.11 and Portable NetWare determine a user's effective rights by looking first at trustee assignmens, then at the effective rights allowed to flow down form above by the Inherited Rights Mask.

of source routing: single-route broad-casting, which sends one copy of a packet over one single-route bridge; and all-routes broadcasting, which sends many copies of a packet over every possible route with single-route and all-routes bridges. A sending workstation can use a conventional or an Open Data-Link Interface (ODI) shell.

ROUTE uses the following parameters: BOARD (specifies the number if the Token-Ring board is not the first board installed); CLEAR (rebuilds the routing table when an IBM bridge is down); DEF (sends broadcast messages without listed addresses and single-route broadcasts to all routes); GBR (sends general broadcast messages to all routes); MBR (sends multi-broadcast frames as single-route broadcasts); REMOVE (removes a node address from the routing table after a bridge has gone down, so that another route must be plotted); RSP (specifies that a file server can respond to a broadcast request with Not Required, an All Routes broadcast frame, or a Single Route broadcast frame); TIME (specifies a time pe-

riod between 3 and 255 seconds for automatic rerouting and table updating when an IBM bridge goes down); and UNLOAD (removes source routing).

ROUTEGEN NetWare (v2.2, v3.11, NetWare for Macintosh) program (on the ROUTEGEN diskette) used to generate bridge/router software on the workstation to be used as the *bridge/router*. This process involves selecting either dedicated or nondedicated mode, real or protected mode, network address (for a nondedicated router), number of communications buffers, and the type and configuration of each LAN board and its driver.

NetWare for Macintosh requires protected mode *routers*.

router A connection between two networks that specifies message paths and may perform other functions, such as data compression. The term router or *bridge/router* is sometimes used interchangeably with *bridge* for devices that perform routing functions, and make two networks a single logi-

cal network, accessible by any of the nodes.

NetWare formerly used the term *bridge*, but now prefers *router*. A **local router** has both input and output ports on a single device. On a **remote router**, input and output ports are separate but linked by a wire or cable segment. An **internal router** is installed in a file server. An **external router** is in another computer. An external bridge can be in a *dedicated* computer, which serves only as a bridge, or it can be in a *nondedicated* computer that is also used as a workstation. A NetWare router can operate in **real mode**, meaning that the router either has an 8086 or 8088 processor or uses its 80286, 80386, or 80486 processor as an 8086 or 8088 processor. Real mode uses only MS-DOS base memory of no more than 1MB. A NetWare router with an 80286, 80386, or 80486 processor can also run in **protected mode**, using extended memory for value added processes (VAPs) and for the ROUTER.EXE program that brings up the router.

ROUTER.CFG NetWare configuration file that can be written with an ASCII text editor to customize the router boot process. ROUTER.CFG specifies when value added processes (VAPs) are to be loaded and where they are located (directory path). When placed on the same diskette or in the same directory as ROUTER.EXE, ROUTER.CFG boots the router without further operator input.

ROUTER.EXE NetWare executable file used to boot a *router*.

routing table NetWare table, maintained by a *file server* or *router*, that contains the locations and status of other routers in an internetwork. Each router broadcasts its own status and updates information about other routers every two minutes. If a file server or a bridge/router goes down, the RESET ROUTER (v2.2, v3.11) console command may be executed on each functioning file server. This command initiates a special router request for information from other functioning file servers, allowing the file server to rebuild its routing table immediately, rather than waiting for the next auto-

matic update.

In Portable NetWare, the RROUTER utility is used to regenerate a table when networks are attached over new bridges or file servers.

RPLODI.COM NetWare boot file for Open Data-Link Interface (ODI) workstations allowing remote booting. RPLODI.COM is loaded after LSL.COM and before the LAN driver.

RPRINTER NetWare command line and DOS executable utility which is loaded as a TSR (terminate-and-stay-resident program) and is used to add or remove a network remote printer. Before RPRINTER can be used, the PCONSOLE menu utility must be used to define the printer as a remote printer and assign a queue, and the following line must be added to the CONFIG.SYS file:

```
SPXconnections=50
```

After entering RPRINTER, type the name of the print server and the remote printer number. A screen message confirms the process.

To remove the remote printer, enter the same information, followed by the -r parameter.

RROUTER Portable NetWare Reset ROUTER Table command-line utility that is used by the network administrator to clear the *routing table* and rebuild it after, for example, adding a network on another bridge or file server. RROUTER is also available from the SCONSOLE Transport Utilities Menu, via the Main Menu and the Utilities Menu.

RS-232 Common name for the Electronic Industries Association (EIA) serial interface standard that uses a 25-pin connector. This designation has been superseded by *EIA-232-D*.

RS232 NetWare v3.11 loadable module providing asynchronous communication between a remote console and its file server. This module is loaded after the REMOTE module.

RSETUP NetWare v3.11 menu utility used to make a remote file server boot diskette (high-density). RSETUP sets the working directory from the Change Working Directory screen on the NetWare RMF Setup Menu; cre-

ates or updates a configuration file with the Edit a Configuration screen; and uses the Create Remote Boot Diskette screen to write operating system files, and AUTOEXEC.BAT, AUTO-EXEC.NCF, and STARTUP.NCF files on the boot diskette.

RSPX   NetWare (v3.11, Portable NetWare) loadable module that contains the SPX driver, which allows a workstation to function as a remote console. RSPX must be loaded into the file server after the REMOTE module, which permits workstation access to the file server console.

RTMP protocol Communications protocol used in NetWare for Macintosh.

RX-Net/2 board Novell network board for ARCnet networks; the same as the PS110 (Standard Microsystems Corporation). Configuration includes setting the RAM buffer base address, I/O port address range, interrupt address, workstation address, and network timeout parameter. The configuration is set with the REFERENCE diskette, which should also contain

the options copied from the LAN_DRV_100 diskette.

RX-Net/II board Half-size Novell network board for ARCnet networks; the same as the PC120 (Standard Microsystems Corporation). The interrupt line, the memory buffer address, and the base I/O address must be set on the board.

RXNET.LAN See *TRXNET.LAN*.

NETWARE DECODER

salvage Process of recovering or restoring data after a system goes down, a disk failure occurs, or a user makes an error.

SALVAGE NetWare menu utility used to recover files that have been deleted (erased but not purged) with the DOS DELETE or ERASE command. In NetWare v2.2, files deleted with the last-entered command can be salvaged. Enter SALVAGE, followed by the volume and path of the erased file or files. The utility must be used from the same workstation as the deletion, and no other file can be created or deleted in the same volume before the SALVAGE command is given. The salvaged file is restored to its original directory.

In NetWare v3.11 and Portable NetWare, SALVAGE can be used to salvage or purge deleted directories; it can also be used to restore files to the original directories or to a DELETED.SAV directory. In addi-

tion, SALVAGE can be used to set salvage options, and to view, recover, or purge salvageable files. Files in a deleted directory are retained in its volume's DELETED.SAV hidden directory, from which they can be copied to other directories. The SALVAGE main menu also allows a user to change the current directory and to sort files by deletion date, size, name, and owner. The restored file retains its original rights.

In NetWare v3.11, the amount of time a deleted file must be retained in the volume can be controlled through the SET console command. *Immediate Purge of Deleted Files* can be set to ON or OFF. *Minimum File Delete Time* can be set for as long as seven days.

In some versions of Portable NetWare, NWConfig file tokens can be used to configure the SALVAGE utility: when the *salvage_utility_flag=* token is set to ACTIVE, it saves the number of files specified with *salvage_num_files=* or the

number of bytes specified with *salvage_max_bytes=*.

SAP See *Service Advertising Protocol.*

sapd daemon Portable NetWare daemon that captures SAP (Service Advertising Protocol) traffic and responds to SAP queries (packets that request information about a network's server types). A daemon is a program that runs automatically when needed. The sapd is activated by the *architecture daemon npsd* with the NPSConfig *sap* = ACTIVE file token. It can also be activated by setting the SAP flag to ACTIVE in the SCONSOLE Edit Transport Parameters screen, via the Main Menu, Configuration Menu, and Transport Configuration Menu.

SBACKUP NetWare v3.11 loadable module that controls operation of Server Backup, a product used to back up a file server on a tape drive. SBACKUP is loaded into the host or host/target file server where it reads and interprets requests and activates other Server Backup modules.(See illustration on following page.)

SCONSOLE Portable NetWare utility that serves as the host interface, permitting startup and use of the *processes* that make up the NetWare file server on the host computer. SCONSOLE is used by the network administrator to start up and shut down services, control volumes, and maintain backup/restore and error logs. SCONSOLE is also used to configure the network, including file and print services, NVT and system parameters, and hybrid users. And it allows utility services to be performed.

SCONSOLE is accessed by logging in to the host system (nwadmin) and, if necessary, changing to the directory containing the utility. Enter SCONSOLE at the prompt. The SCONSOLE main menu contains the Administration, Configuration, Statistics, and Utilities menus, plus options to exit the utility and access HELP.

The Administration Menu contains the Startup/ Shutdown, Backup/ Restore, and Error Log submenus. The Transport Configuration submenu (under the Configuration Menu) permits transport parameters, network assignments, and NVT parameters

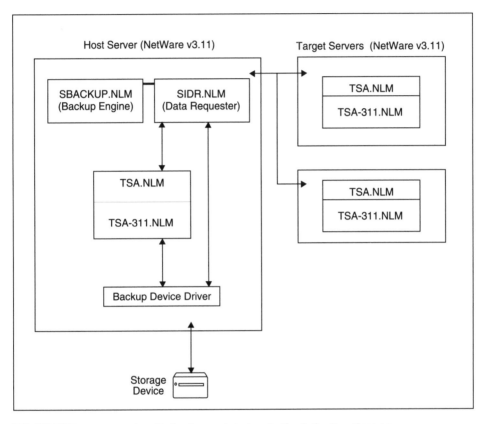

With SBACKUP, one server acts as the "host" server to back up itself and other "target" servers.

to be edited. The Services Configuration submenu contains a File Services Configuration Menu that can be used to edit file services parameters and volume assignments, a Print Services Configuration Menu, a Hybrid User Configuration Menu, and a Security Menu. The Configuration Menu also allows system parameters to be edited.

Many of the network parameters that are stored and set in the NPSConfig and NPConfig files can also be set through SCONSOLE.

script A procedure or command file, as in the UNIX C shell or the Portable NetWare *startnvt* shell script. In NetWare, a **login script** is a user file containing commands for logging in to a network.

SCSI See *Small Computer Systems Interface*.

SDLC See *synchronous data link control*.

Search In NetWare for Macintosh v2.15, the right to see files. In all other versions of NetWare, this right is

called File Scan.

SEARCH NetWare v3.11 console command used to display, add (with the parameter ADD), or delete (DEL) file server search paths for loadable modules and .NCF batch files. The order in which paths are searched can also be specified.

SECURE CONSOLE NetWare v3.11 console command that protects the system against unauthorized entry. The command forbids modules from being loaded from any partition, drive, or directory except SYS:SYSTEM, thus preventing "Trojan horses" (supposedly useful programs containing unauthorized and harmful features). The command allows time and date on passwords, logins, and other features to be changed only by those with Supervisor rights, using the FCONSOLE menu utility. SECURE CONSOLE can also remove DOS from a file server, preventing access to systems that have power-on passwords.

security Prevention of unauthorized en-

try to a computer system or network and its data. Effective security requires determining the access needs of the users and their interaction with the data, and then providing appropriate rights for both the data and the users. Levels of security (called **security classification**) can be determined and assigned to users (**security clearances**), as is done for systems relating to the U.S. government. Effective security also requires methods of preventing unauthorized entry (**external security**) to the system or to data. Locks, passwords, and methods of keeping viruses and other programs from infiltrating the operating system or data (**internal security**) can also be used. A **closed security environment** is one whose operational integrity can be guaranteed by both the system design and the users. An **open security environment** is one in which either the design or a user cannot guarantee operational integrity.

NetWare provides file and directory rights and attributes, and user and group rights. It uses passwords (with the SETPASS command-line utility), locks, and semaphores to pro-

tect network and data security. Rights and attributes are granted and revoked by users with Supervisor rights, and users and groups can be restricted in their ability to log in to the network or use network resources.

SECURITY NetWare command-line utility that allows a user with Supervisor rights to examine the bindery and check for security violations. SECURITY identifies users, groups, and accounts that do not have passwords, and passwords that are the same as the associated usernames. It also identifies the number of users with Supervisor rights, those with access privileges in any volume's root directory, and those with excessive rights in the directories. The information is displayed on the screen and can be redirected (piped) to a DOS file with the following command:

SECURITY >*filename*

It can then be printed with the NPRINT command-line utility.

security equivalences In NetWare, granting a user temporary or permanent use of the same rights or information al-

ready granted to another user. A network supervisor can grant security equivalence to any user. Workgroup Managers and User Account Managers can grant security equivalence to users in their own groups.

semaphore Lock-like feature for multiuser environments that limits the number of tasks or workstations using a file or resource at one time. In NetWare v2.2, information about semaphores is viewed with the FCONSOLE menu utility. Use the File/Lock activity screen to select semaphores.

In NetWare v3.11, the network conditions under which semaphores are handled are defined with the SET console command.

In Portable NetWare, semaphore requests can be viewed with the SCONSOLE File Server Statistics screen, via the Main Menu and the Statistics Menu. Semaphore requests, number of semaphores, and maximum number of simultaneous semaphores can be viewed from the Lock Manager Statistics screen of the Statistics Menu.

shadow directory NetWare directory that contains information about files in a directory, including filenames, attributes, and date when last used.

send As a network node, to originate a message or transfer a message that it has received to the addressee or another intermediate node. A **sender** or transmitting node is a computer or a router, for example.

SEND NetWare command-line utility used to send short messages from a workstation to one or more network users or groups. The message should be included between " " (quotation marks) and followed by the name of the user or group. In NetWare v2.2, v3.11, and Portable NetWare, names should be separated by commas; no commas are used in NetWare Lite. If the users are on another file server, the names should be preceded by the name of the file server and a / (slash).

SEND is also a NetWare v3.11 and Portable NetWare console command used to send a message from a file server to some or all users.

serial transmission Transmitting data one bit at a time, using a standard such as EIA-232-D (formerly RS-232). For instance, a **serial input/output port** supports serial transmission, such as from a computer to a **serial printer**. In MS-DOS and PC DOS, asynchronous serial ports are called COM1 and COM2.

A **serial interface** is hardware that connects devices that use serial transmission.

server or **network server** A network node that provides file management, printing, or other services to other nodes, as in *client/server architecture*. A node can function as a file server exclusively (a **dedicated server**) or it can function as both a file server and a workstation (**a nondedicated server**). A **file server** stores network and data files and provides them to workstations on request. A **print server** performs printing services.

Server Backup NetWare v3.11 software used to back up a file server on a tape drive, view error and backup logs, and restore data. A file server can act as a host, backing up data on other file servers, or it can back up its own data (host/target). The process is controlled by the SBACKUP.NLM loadable module, using the SIDR.NLM module as the data requester and WANGTEK.NLM as the device driver. All modules are loaded in the host file server using the LOAD command, which is followed by the module name and parameters, if any. Each target server or the host/target using the TSA-311.NLM module, which processes the server data, and the TSA.NLM module, which links the SIDR and TSA-311 modules. The Backup Menu and Restore Menu are accessed from the main menu.

Files backed up with Server Backup must be restored with it. The NBACKUP utility is not compatible.

SERVER.CFG File executed during the booting process of NetWare v2.2 The SERVER.CFG file specifies waiting time and other conditions for loading value added processes (VAPs) and enabling an uninterruptible power

supply (UPS). SERVER.CFG is created by a network supervisor at the DOS prompt of a nondedicated file server or DOS workstation.

SERVER.EXE MS-DOS or PC DOS file run at the DOS prompt to boot NetWare v3.11 on a file server. If a STARTUP.NCF or AUTOEXEC.NCF was created during installation, SERVER.EXE executes the file. If neither .NCF file exists, SERVER.EXE brings up the console prompt. SERVER.EXE also mounts the NetWare SYS volume. SERVER.EXE uses the following command parameters: *-S*, followed by the path, if necessary, and the name of a file to be used in place of STARTUP.NCF; *-NA*, used to prevent execution of AUTOEXEC.NCF; *-NS*, used to avoid execution of both STARTUP.NCF and AUTOEXEC.NCF; and *-C cache*, followed by a new cache buffer block size, to change from the default (the new size should also be included in any STARTUP.NCF file).

In NetWare Lite, SERVER.EXE loaded in a workstation permits the workstation to be used as a file server.

server, file See *file server*.

Service Advertising Protocol (SAP) NetWare protocol that determines the type of available network services. In Portable NetWare, the protocol operates as the **sapd daemon**. The daemon is activated by the *architecture daemon npsd* with the NPSConfig *sap* = ACTIVE file token. The SAP can also be activated by setting the SAP flag to ACTIVE in the SCONSOLE Edit Transport Parameters screen, via the Main Menu, Configuration Menu, and Transport Configuration Menu.

Other SAP parameters that can be set with the same SCONSOLE screen include the following: the amount of time before replying to a Get Next Server (GNS) request, the target for SAP standard output, and the target for SAP error messages.

All other versions of NetWare have SAP built in to the operating system.

session The connection between network

nodes for the purpose of data transmission. In the ISO/OSI Reference Model, Layer 5, Session Layer, determines communications paths for transmission.

SESSION NetWare menu utility used to change a file server, log out of a file server, or change its username; display, add, delete, or modify drive mappings; view a list of network groups or send a message to a group; select a new default drive; and view a user list, display information about a user, or send messages to users.

Session layer Layer 5 in the ISO/OSI Reference Model that determines communications paths for transmission.

SET NetWare v3.11 console command used to view operating system parameters and change those parameters that fill the needs of a particular network. Communications parameters govern conditions for watchdog packets (making sure that workstations are connected) and packet receive buffers (for incoming data packets).

Memory parameters include the size of the memory poll, cache buffer block size, and memory on EISA bus computers. SET also governs file cache buffers and directory caching. File system parameters control file deletion and purging, amount of volume used, file attributes, number of directory levels, and number of record and file locks. SET parameters also cover the Transaction Tracking System (TTS), password encryption, NCP searches, and server processes.

Enter SET without parameters to view a list of parameter categories. Selecting a category returns the parameters and their current settings. Most of the parameters can be changed with SET by entering the command, followed by the parameter name and value. The new parameters may be saved in the AUTOEXEC.NCF file. However, some parameters must be changed in the STARTUP.NCF file using the INSTALL program: Auto Register Memory Above 16MB, Auto TTS Backout Flag, Cache Buffer Size, Maximum Physical Receive Packet Size, Maximum Subdirectory Tree Depth, and Minimum Packet Receive

Buffers. Other parameters can be changed through AUTOEXEC.NCF, STARTUP.NCF, or SET: Display Spurious Interrupt Alerts, Display Disk Device Alerts, Display Relinquish Control Alerts, and Display Old API Names.

SETDIR Portable NetWare setdir maintenance utility that changes the directory which stores bindery and shadow access file backups. Access the System Administration Menu; then select Package Management Menu, the Portable NetWare Management Menu, the Portable NetWare Maintenance Utilities Menu, and the Bindery Utilities Menu.

SETPASS NetWare SET PASSword command-line utility used to create or change a user's password to the file server. The password can have up to 127 characters. If a user changes the password on one of several file servers to which the user attaches using the same password, SETPASS will inquire whether the new password should be changed for all the file servers (synchronization). It will also explain situations in which a password cannot be synchronized.

In NetWare Lite, the net setpass command can be used to create a password of 15 characters or less.

SET TIME NetWare v2.2 and v3.11 console command used to set the time and date on a file server. Either AM/PM or 24-hour (international or military) time can be set with hour:minute:second. The date can be entered in the U.S. two-digit number format, the month/date/year format, or the full month name, date, and four-digit year format. The date can also be entered in international format with date, full month name, and four-digit year.

SET TIMEZONE NetWare v3.11 console command used to set time zone information for the CLIB (library of C routines) loadable module. To display the current setting, enter the following command:

```
SET TIMEZONE
```

To change a setting, enter the command and a three-letter zone abbreviation (such as EST for Eastern

Standard Time):

```
SET TIMEZONE EST
```

The zone number in hours east or west of Greenwich Mean Time (GMT) can also be entered. For hours west of GMT, use the number, as in the following example:

```
SET TIMEZONE PST8
```

For hours east of GMT, use a + (plus sign) and the number. Daylight time can also be indicated for a standard time zone:

```
SET TIMEZONE PST8PDT
```

SETTTS NetWare v2.2 and v3.11 SET Transaction Tracking System command-line utility used to turn on or off the NetWare TTS capabilities.

Shareable NetWare file attribute (abbreviated S) that allows several users to access a file at the same time. It is usually assigned in combination with the Read Only attribute.

shared memory In Portable NetWare, the amount of virtual memory available to the interprocess communications (IPC) for tracking user accounts, drive mappings, logins, and process information. Shared memory parameters can be viewed and set in the SCONSOLE Edit System Parameters screen, via the Main Menu and the Configuration Menu, and in the File Server Internal Statistics Screen, via the Main Menu and the Statistics Menu. Shared memory is also addressed in the NWConfig *shm_access*, *shm_key*, and *shm_size* file parameters.

shell A portion of a program that responds to user commands; also called a *user interface*. The shell is loaded as a TSR (terminate-and-stay-resident program). The shell evaluates application requests and either turns them over to DOS for local handling or passes them to the file server for handling by the NetWare Core Protocol (NCP). The shell also tracks the workstation's file server connections, drive mappings, and NCP requests. In addition, the shell program is closely connected to the IPX (which assigns addresses to packets) and SPX (which verifies transmission) communication protocols and to the network board's LAN driver (for

controlling transmissions through the board). The DOS shell and the various shells developed for UNIX, including the Bourne, C, and Korn shells are examples of shells in operating systems.

A NetWare workstation uses one of three **shell files**, NET-*x*.COM, EMSNET*x*.EXE, or XMSNET*x*.EXE, depending on the workstation memory size and management. NET*x*.COM contains the operating system shell for computers using the 1MB of base memory provided by MS-DOS and PC DOS. (The *x* in NET*x*.COM stands for the version of DOS, such as NET4.COM with DOS version 4.x.)

If *expanded memory* is used, the NetWare shell file is EMSNET*x*.EXE. For *extended memory*, the shell file is XMSNET*x*.EXE. (See illustrations on following page.)

SHELL.CFG NetWare shell configuration file that can be created with a text editor and used to customize the parameters a workstation is given through the NetWare *shell* for managing its interactions with the network, including data transmission packet handling, print jobs, and search drives. The file includes parameters used by IPX.COM, EMSNET*x*.EXE, NET*x*.COM, and NETBIOS.EXE.

SHGEN.EXE Portable NetWare executable file used on a workstation during installation of a network to generate the IPX.COM file (internetwork communications protocols). SHGEN is used after the network board has been installed. It is copied from the DOS/ DOS ODI WORKSTATION SERVICES diskette and stored in a user-created directory named NETWARE and its subdirectory SHGEN-1. After starting the file with the SHGEN command, select the LAN driver options. SHGEN will then generate IPX.COM.

In NetWare v2.2 and v3.11, WSGEN.EXE provides this function.

SHIFT NetWare login script command that changes the order in which command-line variables are used. This permits, for example, creation of a list of applications, specifying an application other than the default application

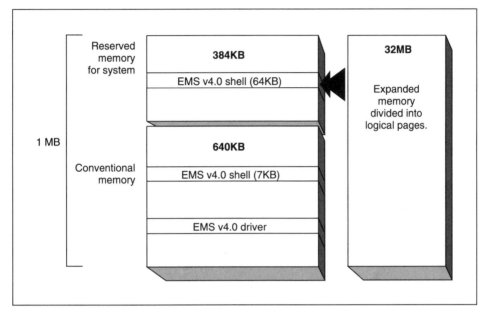

This diagram shows where the expanded NetWare shell fits into memory.

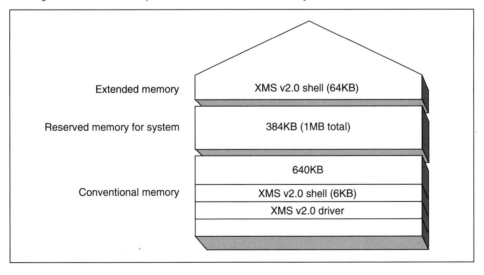

This diagram shows how the NetWare shell fits into extended memory.

to be opened after login without rewriting the script. To access the second application in the list instead of the first one, the command would be:

```
SHIFT 1
```

short machine name or **type** A workstation name used in NetWare overlay files such as CMPQ$RUN.OVL (which specifies screen palette colors). A short machine has no more than four characters, such as IBM, and is identified as SMACHINE in NetWare *login scripts*.

SIDR NetWare v3.11 loadable module that serves as the data requester in a host or host/target file server running the Server Backup software used to back up data on a tape drive. SIDR requests data from a target file server through the TSA module. SIDR is loaded into the host with the LOAD command.

signal-to-noise ratio In signal transmissions, the ratio of the message signal to the random and unwanted signals (noise) that distort the message. The ratio can be expressed as a function of

the system's bandwidth (frequency range).

slave See *guest*.

SLIST NetWare ServerLIST command-line utility that provides information about internetwork file servers. The command provides a list of file servers including, for 80386 file servers, the name, internal network number, node address, and status. The name, network number, and node address are given for 80286 file servers. For information about a single file server, enter SLIST followed by the file server name.

Small Computer Systems Interface (SCSI) Set of hardware and software standards for connecting computers with printers and other peripheral devices. SCSI (pronounced "scuzzy") ports and cabling are provided in Apple Macintosh computers. The interface is available on IBM and compatible computers as a **SCSI bus** or as a board installed in an expansion slot.

SS S S

SMACHINE See *short machine name.*

SMODE NetWare Search MODE command-line utility that defines a program's method of looking for a data file. Eight search modes are possible. Mode 0 indicates that no search instructions other than those in SHELL.CFG will be used. Mode 1 indicates that the path is specified in the executable file, or else the file will search the directory and all search drives. Mode 2 means the path is specified in the executable file, or else the file will search only the directory.

Mode 3 means the path is specified in the executable file, or else the file will search only the directory and, if a Read Only request, will search the search drives. Mode 5 means that if a directory path is specified, the file searches first the path and then the search drives; if no path is specified, the search goes to the default directory first and then the search drives. Mode 7 means that if the path is specified, the executable file searches the search drives; if the open request is Read Only, the file searches the search drives; if no path

is specified, the search is to the default directory; if the open request is Read Only, the file then searches the search drives. Modes 4 and 6 are not defined.

SNA See *Systems Network Architecture.*

socket See *network numbering.*

software driver See *driver*

Simple Mail Transfer Protocol (SMTP) Communications protocol that is a standard for *electronic mail* systems. SMTP allows two-way communication and is used both with TCP (datagram) and with virtual circuit systems.

SMTP See *Simple Mail Transfer Protocol.*

Software serialized keycard See *uninterruptible power supply.*

source routing IBM data routing method used in IBM Token-Ring Networks. The NetWare ROUTE VAP (v2.2) and NLM (v3.11) are drivers that allow NetWare packets to travel on such networks.

sparse file NetWare file with one or more empty blocks, which the operating system does not save on a disk. However, the NCOPY command-line utility can be used to force such files to be saved.

spawn ahead See *process*.

spawn number See *NVT*.

SPEED NetWare v2.2 and v3.11 console command that displays the file server processor's speed — a value determined by the clock speed in hertz (Hz), the processor type, such as 80386, and the number of memory wait states. For most efficient network use, this number should be set as high as possible. It is available in the computer's documentation.

spine network A network to which workstations and file servers are connected indirectly, through an access network and gateway (internetwork).

splice In data communications, to join separate pieces of wire or cable into a single piece. For example, the wires might be joined with barrel connectors. Generally, the fewer the splices the more reliable the network.

spool To send print jobs to a print server's disk storage prior to printing. Spool is an acronym for Simultaneous Peripheral Operations On Line, meaning printer management. In NetWare, data can be spooled with the CAPTURE command-line utility or the NPRINT command-line utility.

    Spooler assignments translate the printer numbers used in some applications to the print queue mappings used in NetWare. Spooler assignments can be listed, created, or changed with the SPOOL console command and saved for future use by including them in AUTOEXEC.SYS using the SYSCON Supervisor Options menu.

SPOOL NetWare v2.2 and v3.11 console command used to list, create, or change spooler assignments. The command alone lists spooler assignments. To create or change a spooler assignment, include the spool number (0 to 4) and the queue name with the command.

SPX Novell Sequenced Packet eXchange protocol used as the resident protocol in NetWare, along with IPX. SPX is derived from IPX and supervises movement of IPX packets. It tracks packets, requests and sends acknowledgments, and retransmits packets, if necessary. SPX is installed from the SPX.COM file.

In NetWare v3.11, the following SPX parameters can be configured with SPXCONFG (SPX CONFiGuration, which is available as a loadable module, console command, or menu utility): SPX watchdog abort timeout (A = number of ticks), SPX watchdog verify timeout (V = number of ticks), SPX ACK wait time out (W = number of ticks), SPX default retry (R = count), maximum concurrent SPX sessions (S = number), quiet mode (suppresses display of changed settings (Q = 1)), and the help screen (H).

In Portable NetWare, the following SPX parameters can be configured with the SHELL.CFG file options: SPX ABORT TIMEOUT, SPX CONNECTIONS (maximum number of simultaneous workstation connections), SPX LISTEN TIMEOUT, and SPX VERIFY TIMEOUT.

SPXCONFG See *SPX*.

SPXS NetWare v3.11 loadable module that provides SPX protocol services under the STREAMS loadable module.

SQL See *Structured Query Language*.

SS keycard See *uninterruptible power supply*.

stack A data structure organized in a last-in, first-out manner. C and other languages place subroutine variables in stacks, allowing routines to call one another hierarchically. In NetWare, the group of IPX/SPX protocols is organized in a stack.

stacking In Portable NetWare, waiting for available processes, rather than having a process available for each client.

star network Network whose logical topology (design) is in the shape of a

star, with all nodes communicating through a central station.

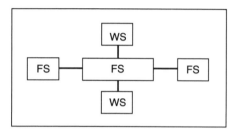

The star network topology connects each workstation to the central server.

start bit In asynchronous serial transmission, a data bit placed in front of the actual data character to indicate the start of transmission.

STARTNET.BAT In NetWare Lite, a batch file that loads LSL.COM, device drivers, IPXODI.COM, and program files. STARTNET.BAT is created with the INSTALL program.

STARTNVT Portable NetWare shell startup script for the Novell virtual terminal. Various NVT tokens are set in the NPSConfig file or with the SCONSOLE utility. STARTNVT is also a utility used; to permit logins that were prevented with the STOPNET utility.

STARTNW Portable NetWare START NetWare utility, which activates the *architecture daemon npsd* and starts the SAP and NWENGINES. These services can also be started through the SCONSOLE Startup/Shutdown Menu, selected from the Main Menu's Administration Menu.

start-stop transmission See *asynchronous transmission*.

STARTUP.NCF NetWare v3.11 boot file that loads disk drivers and name space support. It is executed after SERVER.EXE and before AUTOEXEC.NCF. The file is created in the INSTALL Available System Options Menu.

station restrictions Restrictions on the physical locations from which a NetWare network user can log in. Restrictions can be set in the SYSCON menu utility. Select the User Information Menu, via the Available Topics Menu, and then select the username. Then select Station Restrictions. To

enter a restriction, press INSERT; add network addresses (hexadecimal numbers) in the box.

statistical multiplexing See *asynchronous multiplexing*.

status In data communications, a node's readiness or ability to send or receive data. *Polling*, a method of allowing a workstation to transmit or receive messages, requests the workstation's status.

status reports NetWare reports displayed on the screen that describe or explain network conditions, such as errors, operations, and information.

stochastic Probabilistic. The term is used in data communications to describe the behavior of channels.

stop bit In serial transmission, a bit that follows a character, indicating that transmission is ended. Depending on the protocol, the character can be followed by one or more stop bits or even by fractional stop bits. The lack of the required number of stop bits is called a *framing error.*

STOPNVT Portable NetWare STOP Novell Virtual Terminal command-line utility that prevents logins.

STOPNW Portable NetWare STOP NetWare command-line utility that kills all processes except the *architecture daemon npsd.* These processes can be started through the SCONSOLE Startup/Shutdown Menu, selected from the Main Menu's Administration Menu.

stream Continuous transmission of data. Also, in UNIX a device or file that serves as a continuous data source or destination. In Portable NetWare, a stream is a path between the host and the Portable NetWare processes.

streaming tape Tape storage system that continuously backs up files.

STREAMS NetWare v3.11 loadable module that acts as an interface between NetWare and the network's transport protocols, such as IPX/SPX. STREAMS also requires that the

CLIB, IPXS, SPXS, and TLI modules be loaded.

Structured Query Language (SQL) Programming language developed by IBM that serves as an interface for many types of relational databases on networks and in distributed systems. "Structured" refers to the language's rules of use, such as allowing recursion.

SQL uses three types of command: Data Definition Language, used to create tables and indexes; Data Manipulation Language, used for queries and to add and delete data; and Data Control Language, which grants and revokes database access.

NetWare supports SQL use.

subdirectory See *directory*.

SUPERVISOR In NetWare, the name given to a network supervisor or network administrator when the network is installed; used as a Bindery object. SUPERVISOR is automatically granted Supervisory rights and it cannot be deleted or changed. SUPERVISOR can delegate rights to Workgroup Managers, User Account Managers, File server console operators, Print server operators, and Print queue operators.

Supervisory NetWare v3.11 and Portable NetWare directory security right that grants all other rights in the directory's subdirectories and files. These include the Access Control, Create, Erase, File Scan, Modify, Read, and Write rights. The Supervisory right also supersedes any rights revoked in an Inherited Rights Mask. The Supervisory right can be revoked only on the level at which it was set.

surface test Part of the NetWare INSTALL program that tests a hard disk for bad blocks (disk areas on which data cannot be stored reliably). The test can reformat a disk, destroying any existing data, or it can move data in test areas and then restore the data if the area proves reliable.

switched line A dialed telephone call connection or other communications connection whose path can be different

each time it is made.

SYN See *synchronization*.

synchronization (SYN) In ASCII, synchronization or synchronous idle character (hexadecimal 16, decimal 22) used in synchronous transmission.

synchronous data link control (SDLC) IBM Systems Network Architecture protocol for synchronous transmission. SDLC moves data of any length and code in serial transmission, either full- or half-duplex.

synchronous idle See *synchronization*.

synchronous multiplexing See *time division multiplexing*.

synchronous transmission Continuous data transmission at a constant rate of speed, requiring a synchronization method, such as a header or a sync character. The ASCII SYN (hexadecimal 16, decimal 22) symbol is often used. Synchronous transmission is the method used within a computer and also in high-speed data trans-mission, such as synchronous data link control (SDLC) and binary synchronous communication (BSC).

SYS NetWare volume, created during network installation, that contains the LOGIN, MAIL, PUBLIC, and SYSTEM directories. In NetWare v3.11 and Portable NetWare, the SYS volume also contains the DELETED.SAV directory.

SYSCON NetWare SYStem CONfiguration menu utility used by the network supervisor to control network accounting and information. The Available Topics menu lists Accounting, Change Current Server, File Server Information, Group Information, Supervisor Options, and User Information.

The Accounting option includes installing and removing the accounting feature, setting up and deleting accounting servers, and setting and modifying rates charged to use the network.

The Change Current Server option includes attaching to or logging out of additional file servers, choos-

ing one of the attached servers as the current server, and changing the user's name on the current server.

File Server Information includes the file server name, version of NetWare in use, the system fault tolerance, whether the Transaction Tracking System (TTS) is in use, the maximum number of simultaneous users, the number of current users, and the maximum number of disk volumes on the server.

The Group Information option includes listing the file server's groups; creating, renaming, or deleting a group; viewing, adding, or deleting managed users, managed groups, or managers; assigning or deleting users in a group; viewing a group's ID number; and assigning or modifying a group as a directory trustee, or assigning or modifying its rights in a file.

The network supervisor's options include setting up and changing account balances and restrictions, assigning users' time restrictions, creating or modifying the AUTOEXEC.SYS file, assigning or deleting a file server console operator, activating an intruder detection fea-

ture, creating or modifying the system login script, viewing and erasing the error log, and assigning or modifying the Workgroup Managers.

User Information covers creating, renaming, or deleting users; setting user account balances and restrictions; assigning or changing a password or full name; adding a user to or deleting a user from a group; creating or modifying a login script; copying a login script; viewing or modifying managed users, managed groups, or the list of managers; viewing a user's ID and other login information; assigning or deleting a security equivalence; assigning workstation and time restrictions; assigning or modifying a user as directory trustee or as holding file rights; and limiting a user's disk space.

SYS:DELETED.SAV
See *DELETED-.SAV*.

SYS:LOGIN See *LOGIN*.

SYS:MAIL See *MAIL*.

SYS:PUBLIC See *PUBLIC*.

SYS:SYSTEM See *SYSTEM*.

System NetWare v3.11 security attribute (abbreviated Sy) that allows a file or directory to be hidden during a scan with the DOS DIR (directory) command. Hiding a file or directory prevents it from being deleted or copied. However, it will be listed when the NetWare NDIR command-line utility is used by a user with the File Scan right.

SYSTEM Directory automatically created within NetWare's SYS volume when a network is installed. SYSTEM, which cannot be deleted, contains NetWare utilities that are used only by network supervisors.

Systems Network Architecture (SNA) Three-layer data communications architecture used in distributed mainframe computer systems (IBM). Layers include application, function management, and transmission (control of data link, path, and transmission). SNA is composed of physical units, such as hosts and communications controllers, and logical units

(software). SNA synchronous communication uses the synchronous data link control (SDLC) protocol. The VTAM (virtual telecommunications access method) communications program controls network operations, including access, node connections, data movements, and line and device sharing.

SYSTIME NetWare command-line utility that displays a file server's date and time settings and synchronizes the workstation's date and time settings with those on the server. To display the settings on the default server, enter only SYSTIME. To display the settings on any other attached file server, follow the command with the name of the server.

SYS$LOG.ERR NetWare file containing the error log, in which file server and network error messages are recorded. The file is accessed in either of two ways. For all versions of NetWare, it can be viewed and cleared with the SYSCON menu utility (select Supervisor Options from the Available Topics window, and then

select View File Server Error Log from the Supervisor Options window. To clear the log, press ESCAPE and select YES in the clearing confirmation box.

In Portable NetWare, the file can be viewed, printed, and cleared with options in the SCONSOLE Error Log Menu, via the Main Menu and the Administration Menu.

NETWARE DECODER

T-1 AT&T transmission channel widely used in *time division multiplexing* for high-speed digital transmission of voice and data. T-1 transmits at 1.544 megabits per second.

T-3 AT&T transmission channel used in *time division multiplexing* for high-speed digital transmission of voice and data. T-3 transmits at 44.736 megabits per second.

T-connector Network hardware made up of a barrel connector (which can attache two pieces of cable) that has a third attachment. For example, a BNC T-connector also has a plug for a BNC jack on a network board.

BNC
T-Connector

tag An indicator of an object's attributes, such as ownership, addressing mechanism, meaning, type, size, or state.

TCP/IP Set of widely used protocols (Transmission Control Protocol/Internet Protocol) that covers layers 3 through 7 (Network through Application) of the ISO/OSI Reference Model. The Internet Protocol (IP), which covers Layer 3 (Network layer), defines packets in the form of a *datagram*. The Transport and Session layers (3 and 4) use both the User Datagram Protocol (UDP), which provides unreliable connectionless packet delivery service and TCP, which provides reliable stream delivery. TCP/IP is used on Ethernet networks.

NetWare v3.11 provides connectivity to TCP/IP networks with a group of loadable modules. TCPIP, SNMP (Simple Network Management Protocol), and IPCONFIG (for configuring IP) are required. TCPCON (TCP CONsole, which monitors a local or remote node's protocol stack), SNMPLOG (for event logging), and IPTUNNEL (IP driver

that allows communication with NetWare IPX) are optional.

telecommunications The process of transmitting data between points; includes network design, hardware, transmission medium, protocols, and other software.

terminal Keyboard and screen connected to a remote computer or central processor. It can have local processing ability, such as a computer or workstation connected on a network. Or it can be a dumb terminal, without local processing. A terminal connected directly to a file server is called a console.

terminating resistor See *termination*.

termination In signal transmission, the placing of a hardware **terminator** at the ends of a cable or connection, such as a SCSI bus, in order to prevent corruption or echo of the signal. The terminator (also called a **terminating resistor**) simulates a connector, so that the signal behaves as if it is continuing to another cable segment.

TFTP See *Trivial File Transfer Protocol*.

thin Ethernet See *10BASE2*.

thin/thick Ethernet Ethernet network that uses both thin and thick coaxial cable.

thick Ethernet See *10BASE5*.

tick Time unit used in NetWare data transmission. IBM and compatible computers measure 18.21 ticks per second.

TIME NetWare v2.2 and v3.11 console command that displays the time and date used by the file server. To change the time, use the SET TIME console command.

time division multiplexing Method of transmitting more than one high-speed signal at the same time by sending them at different times, such as interleaving or alternating bits, characters, or messages.

time identifier variables In NetWare login scripts, time variables used with the IF...THEN (v2.2) or IF...THEN...ELSE (v3.11, Portable

NetWare) command. The variables include the following: AM_PM, GREETING_TIME (morning, afternoon, or evening), HOUR (AM or PM number), HOUR24, MINUTE, and SECOND.

timeout In NetWare, the amount of time the system waits before performing an operation, such as loading a module, or before abandoning an operation, such as waiting for a connection or an acknowledgment. Depending on the operation, the time may be measured in seconds or in *ticks*.

time-sharing Use of a computer by several users at the same time without apparent delays in services to any user. Distributed systems and local area networks are examples.

TLI NetWare v3.11 Transport Layer Interface loadable module that provides TLI communication services as part of the STREAMS system (which provides communication between NetWare and the network's transport protocols, such as IPX/SPX). In addition to the STREAMS and TLI

modules, the CLIB, IPX, and SPX modules must be loaded.

TLIST NetWare command-line utility that displays the list of users and groups (trustees) who have been granted rights in a directory or file on an attached file server. To use TLIST, the user must have the Access Control right in the directory. Enter the command and, if necessary, the path or drive mapping to display a list of both users and groups. The USERS or GROUPS option will display only the particular subgroup. Enter two periods (..) to display trustees of the directory above the current directory.

token bus network Bus network that permits a station to transmit messages only when a token has been passed to it. After transmitting, the station passes the token to the next specified station.

TOKEN.LAN LAN driver that links NetWare to a PC Adapter II, 16/4 Adapter, 16/4 Adapter /A, or PC Adapter /A Token-Ring network

board. TOKEN.LAN can be used on both ISA and Micro Channel file servers. The driver is loaded into the operating system with the following command:

```
LOAD TOKEN
```

The command can be followed by the drive letter or volume name and directory path and the driver name and parameters. All parameters are optional. Users can set the board name, node number, unique memory address, and transmit buffer size. Other options should be set by a programmer.

token passing In network communications, a method of allowing a station to transmit data when it holds a **token** (data pattern with an agreed-upon value) that circulates among the stations. Token passing is a feature of Token-Ring networks.

token ring network Ring network that permits a station to transmit messages only when a token has been passed to it. An outgoing message is attached to the token and removed at the receiving end. The receiving sta-

tion can then attach a message to the token and pass it on, or simply pass the token. One implementation is the IBM Token-Ring network.

TOKENRPL NetWare v3.11 loadable module used to remotely boot diskless and other workstations with Token-Ring network boards. After loading TOKENRPL, it should be bound to the LAN driver on the file server with the following command:

```
BIND TOKENRPL
```

The command should include the LAN driver name and any parameters.

This same information must be added to the AUTOEXEC.NCF file using the INSTALL program. Enter the following lines, including the LAN driver name and parameters:

```
LOAD TOKENRPL
BIND TOKENRPL
```

topology The design of a communications network. Two kinds of topology are available. **Logical topology** is the set of protocols incorporating the configuration, such as *star*, *ring*, or *bus*; the method of allowing transmission, such as contention or token passing;

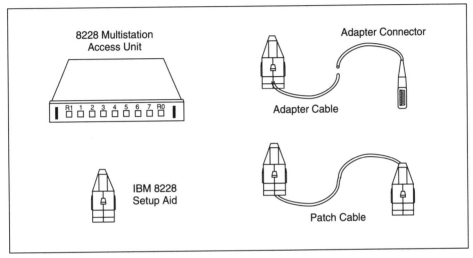

These are the components of a Token-Ring network.

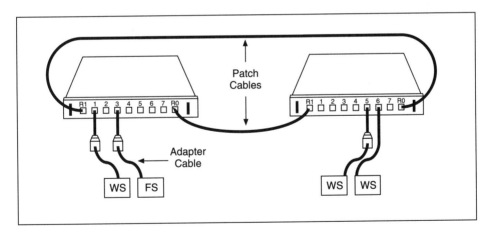

Shown here is the basic layout of a token-ring network.

and other features, such as multiplexing. **Physical topology** is the design for the assembly of computers, other devices, wiring, and other equipment.

TRACK OFF NetWare v2.2 and v3.11 console command that turns off the Router Tracking Screen, preventing display of advertising packets. In Portable NetWare, this command is issued through the TRACK command-line utility, followed by the OFF option.

TRACK ON NetWare v2.2 and v3.11 console command that turns on the Router Tracking Screen, allowing display of advertising packets. Information is displayed about the file server, the network, connection requests, and incoming and outgoing information.

In Portable NetWare, this command is issued through the TRACK command-line utility, followed by the ON option.

track zero test See *ZTEST*.

transaction A series of data management operations handled as a unit, for instance, in a database. Unless all operations are completed, the system is *rolled back* to the condition before the transaction began. In NetWare, transactions are tracked with the *Transaction Tracking System (TTS)*.

Transactional NetWare v2.2 and v3.11 security file attribute (abbreviated T) which indicates that the files are protected by the Transaction Tracking System (TTS) and transaction *backing out* or *rollback*.

Transaction Tracking System (TTS) NetWare v2.2 and v3.11 protection system for bindery files and other database files. TTS monitors transactions and backs out of (rolls back) transactions that are incomplete because of hardware or software failure, error, or user preference. TTS monitoring can be assigned with the Transactional file attribute; it can also be activated in other files when a physical or logical **lock** is placed, indicating that a transaction is in process (**implicit transaction**). Btrieve has built-in backing out. Some ap-

plications have TTS *calls*.

A record of TTS status is kept in the TTS$LOG.ERR file, which is stored in the root directory of the SYS volume.

TTS works by making a copy at the beginning of a transaction and at each step of the transaction. Backing out is possible until TTS marks the transaction as completed, for example, by a release of locks. It works with single- and multiple-user transactions taking place on one or several workstations.

TTS is set with the SETTTS command-line utility. (See illustration on following page.)

transceiver Communications device that operates as both a TRANSmitter and a reCEIVER.

transformer Device that receives alternating-current electrical power from building wiring and changes its voltage so it can be used by another device, such as a network component.

translator unit Communications device that receives network signals, shifts them to higher frequencies, and broadcasts them to the designated workstations. Translator units are used, for example, in IBM PC broadband networks.

transmission In networking, the sending of an electrical signal between points so that it is acknowledged as being accurately received. A **transmission error** is incorrect transmission. Causes of transmission error include variations in the electrical current, signal attenuation, echo (signal reflection), hardware problems, and environmental conditions. Error checking by communications protocols, such as a check digit or checksum, locates packets that are received incorrectly, but does not correct the causes of error.

Transmission Control Protocol/Internet Protocol See *TCP/IP*.

transparent mode Packet transmission that allows control characters and other nondata information to pass through without recognition. The transparent mode can be initiated with

Step 1: TTS searches backward through the transaction work file to find any original data records involved in the aborted transaction.

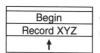

Begin	**Transaction Work File**
Record XYZ	**Cache Buffer**
↑	

Step 2: TTS copies the original data from the transaction work file to the original file.

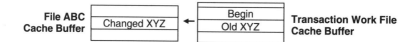

File ABC Cache Buffer | Changed XYZ | ← | Begin / Old XYZ | **Transaction Work File Cache Buffer**

Step 3: Once the original data is written back to disk, TTS writes an "End Transaction" record to the transaction work file.

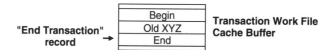

"End Transaction" record → | Begin / Old XYZ / End | **Transaction Work File Cache Buffer**

How NetWare TTS backs out of a partially completed transaction aborted due to workstation failure.

the ASCII *data-link escape character* (DLE).

transport layer In the ISO/OSI Reference Model, Layer 4, Transport layer, assures the reliability of the data being transmitted. This layer is also called the "host-host" layer. Protocols using this layer include the TCP/IP User Datagram Protocol (UDP), which provides connectionless packet delivery, and Transmission Control Protocol (TCP), which provides stream delivery. In NetWare, the SPX protocol performs Transport layer functions.

Trivial File Transfer Protocol (TFTP) Communications protocol used with small systems, sending and receiving messages. TFTP is part of the TCP/IP protocols, operating as part of the Application and Presentation layers. It is based on the TCP/IP Session and Transport layer UDP protocol.

trunk cable Network cable consisting of all the *trunk segments* and their repeaters.

trunk segment A network cable that connects workstations without requiring a *repeater* to strengthen the signal. If all workstations are on a single trunk segment, the segment is also called the *trunk cable*. A larger network trunk cable connects several trunk segments that are joined by repeaters.

trusted In network and data security, a program, system, or network that is guaranteed not to allow security breaches, even though security rights (privileges) make them possible. An example of a trusted network is one designed with the specifications in the U.S. Department of Defense and National Security Agency *Red Book*. Trusted networks rely on both internal design and accurate administrative data (a **"trusted computing base"**).

These two agencies use a seven-level cumulative system, called **Trusted Computer System Evaluation Criteria**. They begin with Minimal Protection (D), and then progress to Discretionary Security Protection (C1), Controlled Access Protection

(C2), Labeled Security Protection (B1), Structured Protection (B2), Security Domains (B3), and Verified Design (A1). When applied to networks, these criteria are called **trusted network interpretation**.

trustee In NetWare, a user or group that is eligible to be granted **trustee rights** in a directory or file. For any specific directory or file, the trustee can be granted all, some, or none of the rights available. Trustee rights in a directory or file (called **trustee assignments**) are granted by the network supervisor or by a user, such as a Workgroup Manager, who has been granted the Access Control right. Trustee rights are not the same as effective rights to use a particular file or directory. Effective rights must also take into account the directory's or file's rights in a Maximum Rights Mask (v2.2) or Inherited Rights Mask (v3.11, Portable NetWare).

TRXNET.LAN LAN driver that links NetWare to an RX-Net, RX-Net II, or PS110 ARCnet network board.

TRXNET can be used on both ISA (AT bus) and Micro Channel file servers. The driver is loaded into the operating system with the following command:

```
LOAD TRXNET
```

The command can be followed by the drive letter or volume name and directory path and the driver name and parameters. An ISA server requires the following parameters: unique interrupt number, unique memory address, and unique I/O port. Board name and number of retries are optional parameters. Micro Channel servers do not have any required parameters. Unique interrupt, unique memory address, and unique I/O port parameters are set with the computer's setup or reference program. Optional parameters include unique board name, number of retries, and board slot number.

TSA.NLM NetWare v3.11 loadable module for target servers in the Server Backup system. TSA links the data requester in the SIDR module with the target-specific TSA-311 module.

TT T T

TSA-311.NLM NetWare v3.11 loadable module in the Server Backup system for a specific target server. TSA-311 uses the server's own data structure for processing data.

TTS See *Transaction Tracking System.*

TTS$LOG.ERR NetWare file that contains a log of Transaction Tracking System (TTS) initializations, disablings, and the transactions it has rolled back. The file is located in the root directory of the SYS volume. It is never deleted or shortened by the operating system, although this can be done by the network supervisor.

tty handler In UNIX, a component that manages data communications with terminals (called **ttys**). UNIX also has a receiver that behaves like a tty file (called *pseudo tty*), which is used by Portable NetWare clients running terminal emulation software.

turbo FAT See *file allocation table.*

turnaround time In half-duplex communications, the amount of time the computer, modem, and other parts of the system need to change the direction of transmission.

twisted-pair Telephone wire also used in network connections. It consists of a pair of individually insulated conducting wires twisted around each other. The insulated wires can be covered with a metal shield to reduce coupling between the conductors, which would generate an electrostatic field, or they can be unshielded. Either shielded or unshielded wire can be used in *10BASE-T* Ethernet networks.

   Twisted-pair cable is a group of twisted-pair wires, such as 4 or 25, bound by a protective covering.

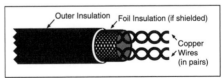

These are the standard parts of twisted-pair cable.

twisted-pair Ethernet See *10BASE-T.*

two-way simultaneous operation A synonym for *full duplex.*

NETWARE DECODER

U2D Portable NetWare UNIX-to-DOS command-line utility that converts UNIX host text files into MS-DOS text files, principally by adding MS-DOS line feeds at line ends. U2D works on either a host or a station.

unbind In network communications, removing the binding or link that connects an object name with a particular network address. In NetWare v3.11, to unbind is to remove the link between an installed network board's communications protocol and its software LAN driver. The console command is UNBIND. The command is followed by the names of the protocol and the LAN driver, and by parameters (if necessary).

In Portable NetWare, unbinding is performed in the BIND heading in the NET.CFG workstation configuration file.

ULIST NetWare Lite command, net ulist, that displays the names and addresses of currently connected network users.

umask UNIX C and Bourne shell command that allows the access (privilege) mode mask for files and directories to be set. The mask governs the read, write, and execute modes.

uninterruptible power supply (UPS) An auxiliary power supply, usually battery operated, that provides reliable electricity to a file server, workstation, bridge, router, or other network device when normal building-supplied electricity is interrupted of fails. The UPS allows the network device to close files and otherwise shut down the system. An **online UPS** receives the electric current as it comes from the building line and reshapes the current into a "clean" (smooth) wave. An **offline UPS** monitors the normal power supply, becoming active only during a transient or other unacceptable change in the current.

After a Novell-approved UPS is installed in an ISA (AT bus) file server, it can be monitored via a

board in an expansion slot. Acceptable monitor boards include the AT-compatible HBA (DCB) or equivalent, a standalone monitor board, and a software-serialized (SS) keycard (required for NetWare v2.2). On a Micro Channel file server, the UPS can be monitored through the mouse port.

In NetWare v2.2, monitoring can begin when the file server is booted if the UPS TYPE command and the hardware type are added to the SERVER.CFG file.

In NetWare v3.11, the UPS module can be loaded when the file server is booted, providing automatic monitoring. To provide automatic monitoring, add the LOAD UPS command to the AUTOEXEC.NCF file. The command should be followed by the name of the board, port number, number of minutes the power supply can function on battery, and number of minutes required to recharge the battery. The UPS module can also be loaded individually, rather than through AUTOEXEC.NCF.

In NetWare v3.11, the status of a UPS can be checked with the UPS STATUS console command. The amount of time the power supply can function and the amount of time needed to recharge the battery can be changed with the UPS TIME console command.

UNIX Multi-user computer operating system through which Portable NetWare can provide network services, running as a set of host computer processes. UNIX is closely tied to the C language. UNIX was developed by AT&T Bell Laboratories and comes in two major versions. System V is supported by AT&T and Berkeley is supported by the University of California, Berkeley. Access to UNIX is provided by shells or interfaces, including the Bourne, C, and Korn shells.

UNIX-to-UNIX Copy Program (UUCP) Transport protocol for file transfer, remote execution of commands, and electronic mail systems over telephone lines. Commands are executed locally after the session is terminated. UUCP-based electronic mail systems are national, international, and world-

wide in scope.

UUCP is also available for the VMS (for Digital Equipment Corporation VAX computers) and MS-DOS operating systems.

unknown request A request for a numbered NetWare Core Protocol (NCP) that is not listed in a file server. NetWare keeps track of how many unknown requests are made. In Portable NetWare, this statistic can be viewed in the SCONSOLE File Server Statistics screen, via the Main Menu and Statistics Menu.

UNLOAD NetWare v3.11 console command that removes a module that was entered into the system with the LOAD console command. UNLOAD is used to remove old LAN drivers to allow installation of new ones. Unloading a LAN driver also unbinds it from its protocol. If a LAN driver has been loaded more than once, it should be removed from a single board with the UNBIND console command, rather than UNLOAD, so that the LAN driver will not be unlinked from the remaining boards.

UNLOAD is also used to remove name space modules and disk drivers. All volumes using a name space module (used to store non-DOS files) should be dismounted before UNLOAD is executed. The volumes cannot be remounted until the module is loaded again. Before unloading a disk driver, all volumes stored on the disks should be dismounted; if this is not done, the operating system will dismount them.

unlock To release a *lock* (exclusive use or ownership) placed on a workstation, system, directory, or file that prevents others from using it.

UNMIRROR NetWare v2.2 console command that turns off the *mirroring* or *duplexing* of a dedicated file server. To use, enter the command and the drive number.

unpadding Removal of characters, such as nulls or zeros, that have been added to data to fill up a fixed-length field or other structure (*padding*).

UPGRADE NetWare v3.11 menu utility

that preserves rights, attributes, and bindery objects when a file server is upgraded from NetWare v2.2 to v3.11. UPGRADE also replaces the Maximum Rights Mask with an Inherited Rights Mask that allows all rights to be inherited.

upload To transmit data from one computer to another, usually a more complex one. An example is uploading a file from a personal computer to a workstation.

UPLOAD NetWare v2.2 utility that transfers NetWare installation files from the SYSTEM-1 diskette to a hard disk. To use UPLOAD, first use the DOS MD command to create a subdirectory called NetWare; then use the DOS CD command to change to that directory. Enter the UPLOAD command to transfer the files.

UPS See *uninterruptible power supply.*

UPS STATUS NetWare v3.11 console command that allows the status of an uninterruptible power supply to be checked.

UPS TIME NetWare v3.11 console command that allows a network supervisor to change the amount of time an interruptible power supply can function, using the following command:

UPS TIME Discharge =

The command should be followed by the number of minutes.

The command can also be used to change the amount of time needed to recharge its battery:

UPS TIME Recharge =

The command should be followed by the number of minutes.

user Individual who is permitted to log in to a NetWare network, having been assigned a **username** of no more than 47 characters. A user can also be listed as part of a group and use the rights assigned to the group. All users are part of the group EVERYONE; they can be assigned to other groups, as well.

user account See *accounting.*

user account manager See *account manager.*

USERDEF NetWare USER DEFinition menu utility that can be used to add users to the network and restrict users' disk space. The command can also be used to edit and view a template (provided in the utility) for adding users, or substitute a created template. To add users, the network supervisor must set up *user accounts* and edit or write *login scripts*. USERDEF is similar to MAKEUSER, but it uses a template instead of directly creating a .USR file.

Before using USERDEF, the SYSCON accounting feature must be installed. In addition, the PRINTCON menu utility must be used to create print job configurations for SUPERVISOR, so that the configurations can be copied; the PRINTDEF menu utility must be used to copy print device definitions.

user ID In NetWare, a hexadecimal number that identifies a user in the bindery and acts as the user's electronic mailbox name (in the SYS:MAIL directory). The network supervisor is always assigned number 1; all other user ID numbers are randomly assigned.

user identifier variables In NetWare login scripts, user variables used with the IF...THEN (v2.2) or IF...THEN...ELSE (v3.11, Portable NetWare) command. The following variables can be used: FULL_NAME (as given in SYSCON files), LOGIN_NAME, and USER_ID.

USERLIST NetWare command-line utility that allows users to view information about the file server's current users, including connection number, login time, network address, and node address. This information is available with the /Address option. The /Object option presents the object type of the connection number. The /Continuous option scrolls the list, rather than stopping at the bottom of each screen.

username See *user.*

USR file See *MAKEUSER; USERDEF.*

UUCP See *UNIX-to-UNIX Copy Program.*

USERS folder NetWare for Macintosh

folder created by the network supervisor in the SYS volume (root directory). The USERS folder contains a folder for each user. When SYS is opened, the desktop displays the USERS folder along with the PUBLIC, LOGIN, MAIL, and SYSTEM folders. The file of an individual user can be opened only by the user and the network supervisor.

utility A computer program or routine that performs file management, data transfer, print formatting, or other functions for an operating system, application, or user. In NetWare, utilities are programs that add functions to the operating system by being added to the file server, workstation, or router. They can be in the form of console commands, including screen commands, installation, maintenance, and configuration commands; NetWare v2.2 value added processes (VAPs); and NetWare v3.11 loadable modules (NLMs), including LAN and disk drivers, and file server enhancements. Command-line (workstation) utilities cover rights, attributes, paths to directories and volumes, file

management, user information, and network administration. Menu utilities, such as COLORPAL, FILER, MAKEUSER, SESSION, SYSCON, and USERDEF, have comprehensive functions.

NETWARE DECODER

value-added process (VAP) NetWare v2.2 application that works as a utility, providing network functions. VAPs can be loaded onto the file server automatically during the booting process if the network supervisor creates a SERVER.CFG file and places it in the SYS:SYSTEM directory. The VAP WAIT command can be used to indicate the number of seconds (between 10 and 300) the file server will wait before loading VAPs. This allows the operator to press any key to abort VAP loading.

VAPs to be run on a router should be copied onto the boot diskette used for the network router. If placed in the same directory as the ROUTER.EXE file, the VAPs are loaded automatically. The ROUTER.EXE file provides a VAP WAIT command for a period of between 10 and 360 seconds. The file's VAP DISK command is used to specify the path to the VAP files.

To use NetWare for Macintosh with NetWare v2.2, VAPs (containing AppleTalk transport protocols, AppleTalk Filing Protocol (AFP) for file services, and AppleTalk print services) are run on a NetWare file server or router called the **VAP host**. These VAPs allow the file server or router to be a node on an AppleTalk network. Configuration VAPs are also provided for use during installation of NetWare for Macintosh.

The NetWare v2.2 VAP console command displays a list of loaded VAPs (and their commands).

VAP See *value-added process.*

VER NetWare v2.2 console command that displays the version of NetWare running on the file server.

verification, data Method of assuring that data has been transferred accurately between nodes or from a processor's RAM to disk storage. In data communications, protocols are designed to

provide verified transmission over channels that may carry unwanted signals (noise) and with hardware that operates at different speeds and different degrees of accuracy.

In NetWare, **read-after-write verification** is a method of data verification in which data that has just been saved on a disk is immediately compared with the data in the processor's memory (RAM). If the data doesn't match, it is redirected to another disk area called the *Hot Fix Redirection Area*. (See illustration on following page.)

VERSION NetWare command-line utility that displays the software version, copyright information, and checksum of a NetWare executable (.EXE) file. The VERSION command is followed by the path, if necessary, and the filename (the .EXE extension does not need to be entered).

In NetWare v3.11, VERSION is also a console command that displays similar information about the file server.

vertical parity See *parity*.

vertical redundancy check (VRC) In data transmission, a method of error detection in which each character contains a parity bit; all characters are checked for either odd or even *parity*.

virtual telecommunications access method (VTAM) IBM software for System/370 mainframe networks that provides network control and sharing, allocates resources, controls access, and moves data.

voice grade channel Communications channel for voice or data with a frequency range of approximately 300 to 3,000 hertz.

VOLINFO NetWare VOLume INFOrmation menu utility that displays information about each volume in a file server. The command alone provides information about the current server, including its name, total number of kilobytes or megabytes, number of free kilobytes or megabytes, the number of directory entries allocated, and the number of available directory entries.

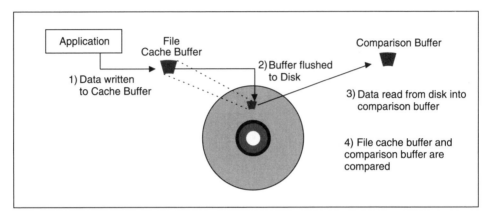

NetWare retains a copy of the written data in its memory and compares the data on the disk to the copy in memory. If the two copies don't match, the read-after-write verification fails.

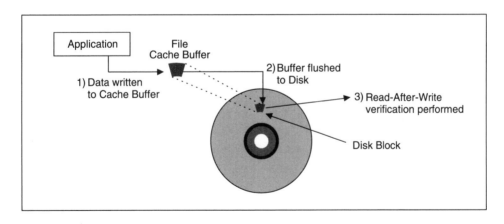

NetWare's read-after-write verification occurs when the cached data is flushed to disk, rather than when the data is written to cache.

To view the same information about another file server, select Change Servers from the Available Options menu and select the file server. If the user is not attached to the server, enter the username in the New User Name entry box. If a password is required, enter it in the Password entry box. The server can then be selected.

The Update Interval option allows the network supervisor to adjust the amount of time between automatic updates of volume information, specifying a number between 1 and 3,600 seconds. (See illustration on following page.)

volume NetWare name for an amount of named storage space on a hard disk, allocated when the network is installed. The operating system automatically creates the SYS volume, along with the SYSTEM, PUBLIC, LOGIN, and MAIL directories. In NetWare v3.11 and Portable NetWare, the system also creates the DELETED.SAV hidden directory. SYS and its directories cannot be deleted or renamed.

At the time of installation, other volumes can also be created and defined. Any later changes in volume characteristics, such as size, will destroy all existing data and structures.

A volume's data is stored in up to 32 **volume segments**, which can be located on one or more hard disks. Additional segments can be added to an existing volume by adding a hard disk with a NetWare partition, and then designating new volume segments. This process does not require disruption of volume use.

A volume's name, size, and disk location are saved in its **volume definition table**.

In NetWare for Macintosh, a volume is represented on the desktop by a **volume icon** that looks like an open, two-drawer filing cabinet. If a volume is located on a file server running NetWare v2.2, the cabinet has one lower drawer. If the server is running NetWare v3.11, the cabinet has two lower drawers. As with other desktop icons, double-click to open a volume.

volume restrictions Assignment of NetWare volume space for accounting purposes. Volume restrictions are

```
  Page 1/1        Total    Free      Total    Free      Total   Free

  Volume name         SYS                VOL1
  KiloBytes       30,048    6,496     96,612   95,600
  Directories      2,432    1,390      6,528    6,525

  Volume name
  KiloBytes
  Directories
```

```
            Available Options

            Change Servers
            Update Interval
```

The VOLINFO screen tells you the total space and the space available on each volume.

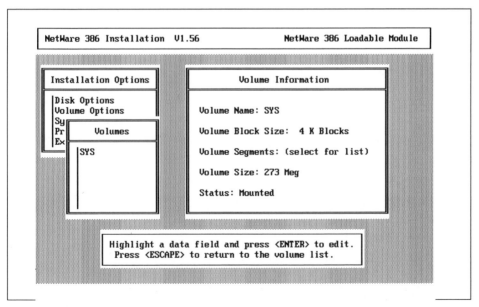

```
  NetWare 386 Installation  V1.56          NetWare 386 Loadable Module

    Installation Options           Volume Information

    Disk Options
    Volume Options            Volume Name: SYS
    Sy
    Pr    Volumes            Volume Block Size:  4 K Blocks
    Ex
       SYS                   Volume Segments: (select for list)

                             Volume Size: 273 Meg

                             Status: Mounted


         Highlight a data field and press <ENTER> to edit.
         Press <ESCAPE> to return to the volume list.
```

When you create a new volume, INSTALL displays a "Volume Information" window, which you can edit to suit your needs.

assigned by the network supervisor or by a designated user account manager who has been assigned file security rights.

VOLUMES NetWare v3.11 console command that lists the names of volumes mounted on the file server.

VRC See *vertical redundancy check.*

VREPAIR NetWare Volume REPAIR v2.2 down command or v3.11 loadable module that is used to recover volume data after a power failure or because of a disk defect. In NetWare v2.2, VREPAIR locates bad blocks in a volume and recovers data from lost blocks (those not recorded in the File Allocation Table).

In NetWare v3.11, VREPAIR locates a volume's bad blocks, including read, data mirror mismatch, multiple allocation, fatal directory, and write errors. VREPAIR can remove or retain name spaces for non-DOS files, write only changed directory and FAT entries or all changed entries, and either store changes for later update or make them available immediately.

VTAM See *virtual telecommunications access method.*

wait state Time period used to synchronize network devices so they are all operating at the same apparent speed. For example, if the central processor is faster than other devices, it waits (does nothing) as a way of slowing down to the speed at which the entire network can operate.

wait time Number of seconds an uninterruptible power supply (UPS) waits before notifying the file server that the normal power supply is no longer available. When notified, the server signals users to log out.

WAN See *wide area network*.

WANGTEK.NLM NetWare v3.11 loadable module that contains the driver for the tape backup unit used in the Server Backup software system. WANGTEK is installed in the host server.

watchdog NetWare packets whose purpose is to assure the connection of a workstation to the file server if it has not received a packet within a certain time. NetWare v2.2 uses the WATCHDOG console command. To set the start value (the amount of time the server waits to check a new connection), follow the command with START= and the number of seconds between 15 and 1,200 (20 minutes). To set the interval value (the time between watchdog packets), follow the command with INTERVAL= and the number of seconds between 1 and 600. To set the count value (the number of intervals before the connection is cleared), follow the command with COUNT= and a number between 5 and 100.

NetWare v3.11 uses the SET console command. The Delay Before First Watchdog Packet parameter can be set between 15.7 seconds and 20 minutes 52.3 seconds. The Delay between Watchdog Packets parameter can be set between 1 second and 10 minutes 26.2 seconds. The Number of Watchdog Packets parameter

can be set between 5 and 100.

In Portable NetWare, the NWConfig *log_watchdog-logouts=* ACTIVE file parameter displays each logout by the watchdog.

WHOAMI NetWare command-line utility that displays information about a user's attachments to file servers. The /Security option displays security equivalences. The /Groups option displays a user's membership in *groups*. The /Workgroup option displays *workgroup manager* information. The /Rights option displays a user's *effective rights*. The /SYstem option displays system information. The /Object option displays the network supervisor. The /All option displays all the previous information. In NetWare v3.11, the /Continuous option allows continuous scrolling of the information list.

wide area network (WAN) Communications network that covers a region or a country.

wideband channel Communications channel whose frequency range is greater than the frequency range for a *voice grade channel*.

wildcard In computer terminology, a character with a special meaning that allows it to stand for any digit, character, group of digits or characters, or other specified groupings. The term (more formally a metacharacter) is derived from jokers or other cards that can stand for any card in certain games.

NetWare recognizes two wildcards. An * (asterisk) can be used for any character or characters in a filename. A ? (question mark) can be used in place of a single character in a single position.

window A computer screen area that can be handled independently of the rest of the screen or of another window. Windowing is provided in the Apple Macintosh operating system and is also available with Microsoft Windows and OS/2 Presentation Manager.

In data communications, a window refers to a specific number of packets (or **window size**) that can be sent before receiving an acknowledgment or negative acknowledgment. A

protocol with this capability is called a **windowed protocol**. An example is Windowed XModem (*W/XModem*).

Windowed XModem See *W/XModem*.

wire A drawn metal filament or rod, which may be covered by an insulating material. Telephone or *twisted-pair wire*, which is sometimes used for network connections, consists of a pair of individually insulated conducting wires twisted around each other.

wiring closet See *hub*.

word In computer data, the basic unit of information handled by a computer. Many personal computers use a 16-bit word.

Workgroup Manager Person appointed by a NetWare network supervisor to manage data and users belonging to a *group*. The Workgroup Manager is granted Create and Delete rights for some bindery objects, such as users in one or more groups. In such a case, the Workgroup Manager is also the User Account Manager. A manager who has been granted the appropriate rights can also make or modify trustee directory and file assignments and volume and disk space restrictions. The Workgroup Manager can also be granted Supervisory rights in specified directories or volumes.

The network supervisor can create a Workgroup Manager with the SYSCON menu utility. Select Supervisor Options from the Available Topics menu; then select Workgroup Managers. Press the INSERT key to display a list of possible managers.

workstation identifier variables In NetWare login scripts, user variables used with the IF...THEN (NetWare v2.2) or IF...THEN...ELSE (NetWare v3.11, Portable NetWare) command. The following variables can be used: MACHINE (long machine name), OS (operating system), OS_VERSION, P_STATION (workstation number or hexadecimal node address), SHELL_TYPE (shell version), SMACHINE (short machine name), and STATION (connection number).

write To copy data from computer RAM to a hard disk. Write is also called save.

Write is a NetWare security right (abbreviated W) for directories that grants the right to open and modify files in the directory. In v3.x, Write can also be assigned to individual files.

WRITE is a NetWare login script command that allows a user to enter text for screen display. The text must be between quotation marks (" "), and lines must be separated by semicolons (;). Text can include carriage returns (the symbol \r), new lines (\n), embedded quotation marks (\"), and the beep sound (\7). Strings can also be manipulated with the following operators: concatenation (;), multiply (*), divide (/), modulo (%), add (+), subtract (-), and shift or truncate left (<<) or right (>>).

Write Audit NetWare file security attribute (abbreviated Wa) that is not currently in use.

Write Behind In Portable NetWare, a method of validating saved data before it is considered written on the disk. Write Behind can be set to ACTIVE as a flag from the SCONSOLE Edit File Services Parameters screen, via the Main Menu, Services Configuration Menu, and File Services Configuration Menu. A *write_behind_flag* token can also be set to ACTIVE in the NWConfig file.

write lock A security lock that prevents a file from being modified and, in some systems, from being read.

WSGEN NetWare v2.2 and v3.11 command-line utility used to create the IPX.COM file, which installs the NetWare IPX protocol. WSGEN is executed after the network board has been installed. It is provided on the DOS WORKSTATION SERVICES diskette. To use WSGEN from a hard disk, first create a directory called NetWare; then create a subdirectory called WSGEN. Then copy the file to the WSGEN subdirectory.

To use WSGEN, enter the command; then select the appropriate LAN driver (from the available list or from a supplementary list on the

LAN_DRV_??? diskette) for the installed network board. Also select the LAN driver configuration option. WSGEN will then generate IPX.COM.

In Portable NetWare, this function is provided by SHGEN.EXE.

WSUPDATE NetWare v2.2 and v3.11 command-line utility that allows workstation shells and other files to be updated from the file server. WSUPDATE functions by comparing the date of the source file with that of the workstation file and providing the update if the source file is more recent. Enter the command; include, if necessary, the source path, destination drive, and filename, and any options. The destination drive can be specified by letter, by ALL (for all the workstation's drives), or ALL_LOCAL (for all the workstation's local drives).

WSUPDATE has the following options: /F and the path and filename (for including a command line updating commands in a file); /I (for an individual prompt for each update required), /C (for automatically copying the updated file over the old one), or /R (for renaming the old file before copying the new one); /S (for searching all subdirectories of the drive or drives); /L and the path and filename (for creating a log file); or /O (for updating Read Only files).

W/XModem Windowed XModem, a version of the XModem protocol that allows as many as four packets before receiving an acknowledgment or negative acknowledgment.

NETWARE DECODER

X.25 CCITT communications standard for data handling on packet-switched networks. X.25 contains protocols covering Layers 1 through 3 (Physical, Data-Link, and NetWork) of the ISO/OSI Reference Model. It uses high-level data-link control (HDLC). The standard describes the data terminal equipment/data circuit-terminating equipment (DTE/DCE) interface. X.25 is internationally accepted for wide area networks (WANs).

X.400 CCITT communications standard defining a protocol and specifications for a computer-based message handling system.

X.500 CCITT communications standard for electronic mail, including user directories.

XModem Data communications protocol that sends a *packet* or block consisting of a start of header character, a block number, a one's complement

block number, 128 bytes of data, and a *checksum*. The receiver uses the checksum to verify each packet's accuracy and then sends an acknowledgment. When the sender receives the acknowledgment, it transmits another packet.

XModem 1K See *YModem*.

XMSNET*x*.EXE NetWare file that places most of the NetWare shell in *extended memory;* used in place of the NET*x*.COM shell file, which is used with conventional memory. Extended memory is computer memory above the 1MB ordinarily used by MS-DOS and PC DOS. It is available through third-party software and hardware. One widely available software interface is XMS, eXtended Memory Specification (Lotus, Intel, Microsoft, and AST Research), which requires a device driver or XMM (eXtended Memory Manager).

Using XMSNET*x*.EXE frees approximately 34KB of conventional

memory space; however, some shell functions, such as handling interrupts, remain in conventional memory. XMSNET*x*.EXE works with DOS 3.0 and above (the *x* stands for the version of DOS being used, such as XMSNET4.EXE for DOS 4.01).

The XMSNET*x*.EXE file is loaded after the extended memory driver has been loaded. XMSNET*x*.EXE should be copied to the boot disk and its name included in the AUTOEXEC.BAT file. In NetWare v3.11, XMSNET*x* is available as a command-line utility.

XON/XOFF An asynchronous protocol used in handshaking — the first procedure in establishing a session with RS-232 serial communications. XON/XOFF monitors a receiver's message buffer, sending an XOFF (stop transmission) message flow control character when the buffer is almost full and an XON (resume transmission) character when the buffer is almost empty.

NETWARE DECODER

YModem Communications protocol intended to improve the *XModem* protocol by sending 1KB of data in each block. It also supports batch file or multiple file transfer.

YModem is also known as XModem 1K.

YModem-g Communications protocol, a variant of *YModem*, that transmits without waiting for acknowledgments.

NETWARE DECODER

ZModem Communications protocol intended to improve the *XModem* and *YModem* protocols by employing data streaming, acknowledging a message only when transmission is completed. Transmission errors induce a negative acknowledgment.

zone In the Macintosh network protocol AppleTalk Phase 1, a logical internetwork whose component networks are linked by routers. AppleTalk Phase 2 applies zone to an internetwork whose component networks are attached to a single high-speed cable as is possible, for example, using Ethernet or Token-Ring topology.

ZTEST (track zero test) In NetWare v2.2, a physical test of a hard disk's ability to store data reliably. Running the test on Track 0 destroys any formatting and data already on the disk and it is used only the first time a disk drive is used for NetWare. ZTEST is one of four modules run during the INSTALL program, although it is not required. From the opening screen of the module, run the test by pressing <Enter> or bypass the test by pressing <Escape>. If the test continues, the screen requires a Yes/No response for each available drive. After a test is run, the program grades its performance, blocking installation of a bad disk. In this case, the installation must be halted until a usable disk is placed in service. To exit the ZTEST module, press F10.

APPENDIX A

Numbers & Symbols

1BASE5 Type of IEEE twisted-pair baseband Ethernet that transmits at a rate of 1 megabit per second. 1BASE5 operates over a limited distance and is intended to provide a network cabling system at lower cost than conventional 10BASE-T twisted-pair Ethernet. 1BASE5 uses a star topology and can have multiple layers of hubs. It transmits point-to-point with one twisted-pair as the uplink and one pair as the downlink. Voice and data pairs can coexist in cable bundles.

3C503 EtherLink II 3C503 (3COM) network board for thin Ethernet and thick Ethernet networks. The board controls base I/O address, memory address, and Remote Reset. The settings for interrupt line (IRQ) and connector type settings are installed on the workstation with WSGEN.EXE, on the router with ROUTEGEN.EXE, and on the file server with INSTALL.EXE (NetWare v2.2) or at the colon prompt (NetWare v3.11). The board is com-

patible with NetWare when the 3C503.LAN driver is installed in the operating system.

3C503.LAN LAN driver that links NetWare to a 3C503 (3COM) thin or thick Ethernet network board installed in a file server. The driver loads into the operating system with the LOAD command (NetWare 386). The LOAD command may also include the interrupt, memory address, and unique I/O port number parameters otherwise you will be prompted for each parameter. You can also specify the following optional parameters: frame (packet header), the board's unique name, the node address, and number of transmission retries after failure.

Although the thin Ethernet BNC cable designation is the default, thick cable (DIX) can be specified with the following command:

```
LOAD 3C503 DIX
```

3C505 EtherLink Plus 3C505 (3COM) network board for thin Ethernet and thick Ethernet networks. NetWare supports only Assembly #2012 and only on file servers with less than 16MB of memory. All board settings are hardware controlled. The board is compatible with NetWare when the 3C505.LAN driver is loaded in the operating system.

3C505.LAN LAN driver that links NetWare to a 3C503 (3COM) thin or thick Ethernet network board installed in a file server. The driver is loaded into the operating system with the LOAD command (NetWare 386). You can include the Direct Memory Address (DMA) channel, interrupt, and I/O port. You can also specify the following optional parameters: frame (packet header), board name, node number, and number of retries.

3C523 EtherLink/MC 3C523 (3COM) network board for thin or thick Ethernet networks. The I/O address range, the RAM buffer address, and the number of the slot the board is installed in are set with the computer's setup or reference program.

3C523-TP EtherLink/MC-TP 3C523 (3COM) network board for twisted-pair Ethernet networks. The board controls impedance, DC signal, receive threshold, link beat, equalization, transmit level, and Remote Reset. Interrupts, memory addresses, I/O ports, and transceiver type are set with the computer's setup or reference software.

3C523.LAN LAN driver that links NetWare to a 3C523 (3COM) thin or thick Ethernet network board or a 3C523-TP (3COM) twisted-pair wire Ethernet network board installed in a file server. The driver is loaded into the operating system with the LOAD command (NetWare 386). You can specify the slot number. Frame (packet header), board name, node number, and number of retries are optional parameters.

8-way splitter See *eight-way splitter*.

10BASE2 Type of coaxial cable baseband IEEE Ethernet usually called *thin Ethernet*. 10BASE2 is intended for a departmental or work area network within a large organization, complementing a 10BASE5 (thick Ethernet) network. It transmits over coaxial cable and uses BNC T-connectors. The transmission rate is 10 megabits per second and the minimum medium propagation velocity is 0.65c (c = 3 x 10^8). Maximum cable segment length is 185 m with a maximum medium delay per segment of 950 ns. The mean time between failures is rated at 100,000 hours.

10BASE5 Type of coaxial cable baseband IEEE Ethernet usually called *thick Ethernet*. 10BASE5 is intended for use as a primary backbone for a large organization. It transmits over coaxial cable and uses N connectors. The transmission rate is 10 megabits per second and the minimum medium propagation velocity is 0.77c (c = 3 x 10^8). Maximum cable segment length is 500m with a maximum medium delay per segment of 2,165 ns. The mean time between failures is rated at 1,000,000 hours.

10BASE-T Unshielded twisted-pair baseband IEEE Ethernet, intended to provide low-cost, easy-to-install networking by using telephone building wiring, telephone wiring practices, and BNC connectors. The transmission rate is 10 megabits per second and the minimum medium propagation veloc-

ity is 0.59c (c = 3 x 10^8). Maximum cable segment length is 100m. The network's mean bit error rate at the physical layer is less than 1:100,000,000.

10BROAD36 Type of coaxial cable broadband IEEE Ethernet that uses community antenna/cable-TV coaxial cable (CATV) and connectors.

< Symbol for the conditional expression "is less than" used in the NetWare IF...THEN (v2.2) and IF...THEN...ELSE (v3.11) login script commands.

<= Symbol for the conditional expression "is less than or equal to" used in the NetWare login script commands IF...THEN (v2.2) and IF...THEN...ELSE (v3.11).

= Symbol for the conditional expression "is equal to" used in the NetWare login script commands IF...THEN (v2.2) and IF...THEN...ELSE (v3.11).

== Symbol for the conditional expression "is exactly equal to" used in the NetWare login script commands IF...THEN (v2.2) and

IF...THEN...ELSE (v3.11).

>= Symbol for the conditional expression "is greater than or equal to" used in the NetWare login script commands IF...THEN (v2.2) and IF...THEN...ELSE (v3.11).

> Symbol for the conditional expression "is greater than" used in the NetWare login script commands IF...THEN (v2.2) and IF...THEN...ELSE (v3.11).

!= Symbol for the conditional expression "is not equal to" used in the NetWare login script commands IF...THEN (v2.2) and IF...THEN...ELSE (v3.11).

Symbol for NetWare login script command EXTERNAL PROGRAM EXECUTION, permitting execution of non-login commands, including programs, files, and menus. Begin the command with #, followed by the directory path (including drive letter (in DOS) or NetWare volume name), the name of an executable file (omit the .EXE or .COM extension), and any necessary file parameters.

Also a symbol for the conditional expression "is not equal to" used in the NetWare login script commands IF...THEN (v2.2) and IF...THEN...ELSE (v3.11).

APPENDIX B

ASCII Character Table
Hexadecimal and Decimal

ASCII		Character	
Hex	**Dec**		
0	0	NUL	(null or blank)
1	1	SOH	(start of header)
2	2	STX	(start of text)
3	3	ETX	(end of text)
4	4	EOT	(end of transmission)
5	5	ENQ	(enquiry)
6	6	ACK	(acknowledge)
7	7	BEL	(bell)
8	8	BS	(backspace)
9	9	HT	(horizontal tabulation)
A	10	LF	(line feed)
B	11	VT	(vertical tabulation)
C	12	FF	(form feed)
D	13	CR	(carriage return or enter)
E	14	SP	(shift out)
F	15	SI	(shift in)
10	16	DLE	(data link escape)
11	17	DC1	(device control 1)
12	18	DC2	(device control 2)
13	19	DC3	(device control 3)
14	20	DC4	(device control 4)

ASCII

Hex	Dec	Character	
15	21	NAK	(negative acknowledge)
16	22	SYN	(synchronization)
17	23	ETB	(end of text block)
18	24	CAN	(cancel)
19	25	EM	(end of medium)
1A	26	SUB	(substitute)
1B	27	ESC	(escape)
1C	28	FS	(file separator)
1D	29	GS	(group separator)
1E	30	RS	(record separator)
1F	31	US	(unit separator)
20	32	SP	(space)
21	33	!	(exclamation mark)
22	34	"	(quotation mark)
23	35	#	(pound sign)
24	36	$	(dollar sign)
25	37	%	(percent sign)
26	38	&	(ampersand)
27	39	'	(apostrophe or closing single quote)
28	40	(	(left perenthesis)
29	41	)	(right parenthesis)
2A	42	*	(asterisk)
2B	43	+	(plus sign)
2C	44	,	(comma)
2D	45	-	(hyphen)
2E	46	.	(period)
2F	47	/	(slash)
30	48	0	

ASCII

Hex	Dec	Character	
31	49	1	
32	50	2	
33	51	3	
34	52	4	
35	53	5	
36	54	6	
37	55	7	
38	56	8	
39	57	9	
3A	58	:	(colon)
3B	59	;	(semicolon)
3C	60	<	(less than)
3D	61	=	(equal sign)
3E	62	>	(greater than)
3F	63	?	(question mark)
40	64	@	(at sign)
41	65	A	
42	66	B	
43	67	C	
44	68	D	
45	69	E	
46	70	F	
47	71	G	
48	72	H	
49	73	I	
4A	74	J	
4B	75	K	
4C	76	L	
4D	77	M	

ASCII		Character
Hex	**Dec**	
4E	78	N
4F	79	O
50	80	P
51	81	Q
52	82	R
53	83	S
54	84	T
55	85	U
56	86	V
57	87	W
58	88	X
59	89	Y
5A	90	Z
5B	91	[(left bracket)
5C	92	\ (backslash)
5D	93	] (right bracket)
5E	94	^ (caret or circumflex)
5F	95	_ (underscore)
60	96	' (opening single quote)
61	97	a
62	98	b
63	99	c
64	100	d
65	101	e
66	102	f
67	103	g
68	104	h
69	105	i
6A	106	j

ASCII		Character	
Hex	**Dec**		
6B	107	k	
6C	108	l	
6D	109	m	
6E	110	n	
6F	111	o	
70	112	p	
71	113	q	
72	114	r	
73	115	s	
74	116	t	
75	117	u	
76	118	v	
77	119	w	
78	120	x	
79	121	y	
7A	122	z	
7B	123	{	(left brace)
7C	124	|	(vertical line)
7D	125	}	(right brace)
7E	126	~	(tilde)
7F	127	DEL	(delete)

APPENDIX C

Netware Commands and Utilities by Function

	v2.2	v3.11	Portable NetWare	NetWare Lite
Configuration Information				
BCONSOLE	x	x		
CHKDIR		x	x	
CHKVOL	x	x	x	
COMCHECK	x	x	x	
CONFIG	x	x		
DISPLAY NETWORKS	x	x		
DISPLAY SERVERS	x	x		
DROUTER			x	
GETLAN			x	
INFO				x
MEMORY		x		
MODULES		x		
MONITOR	x	x		
NAME	x	x		
NDIR	x	x	x	
NDLIST				x
PAUDIT	x	x	x	
PNWSTATUS			x	
PROTOCOL		x		
PSTAT	x			
SLIST	x	x	x	

	v2.2	v3.11	Portable NetWare	NetWare Lite
SPEED	x	x		
TIME	x	x		x
VER	x			
VERSION	x	x	x	
VOLUMES		x		
UPS STATUS		x		
UPS TIME		x		
File Management				
BACKUP	x			
BINDFIX	x	x	x	
BINDREST	x	x		
BROUTER	x	x		
D2U			x	
EDIT		x		
HOLDOFF	x			
HOLDON	x			
NBACKUP	x	x	x	
NCOPY	x	x	x	
NDIR	x	x	x	
PURGE	x	x	x	
REMIRROR	x			
SALVAGE	x	x	x	
SBACKUP		x		
SIDR		x		
TSA		x		
TSA-311		x		
UPLOAD	x			
U2D			x	
WANGTEK		x		

	v2.2	v3.11	Portable NetWare	NetWare Lite
File Server Management				
ACONSOLE		x		
ATTACH	x	x	x	
CONSOLE	x			
DOWN	x	x		
FCONSOLE	x	x	x	
NVER	x	x	x	
RCONSOLE		x	x	
REMOTE		x	x	
REMOVE DOS		x		
RSETUP		x		
RS232		x		
SEARCH		x		
SLIST	x	x	x	
SMODE	x	x	x	
SYSTIME	x	x	x	
VERSION		x		
Help				
HELP	x	x	x	x
Installation				
ADD NAME SPACE		x		
AUTOCFG	x	x		
BIND		x		
DISKSET	x	x		
DOWNLOAD	x			
EMSNETx	x	x	x	

	v2.2	v3.11	Portable NetWare	NetWare Lite
ENABLE LOGIN	x	x		
INSTALL	x	x		
LOAD		x		
MOUNT	x	x		
NETx.COM	x	x	x	
REGISTER MEMORY		x		
SCONSOLE			x	
SEARCH		x		
SHGEN			x	
UNLOAD		x		
WSGEN	x	x		
XMSNETx	x	x	x	
LAN Drivers				
JUMPERS	x	x		
NMAGENT		x		
Macintosh Connections				
APSNLM		x		
APSVAP	x			
ATALK	x	x		
ATALK2	x	x		
MAC.NAM		x		
Network Maintenance				
CFS			x	
CLEAR STATION	x	x		
COMPSURF	x			
DCONFIG	x	x	x	

	v2.2	v3.11	Portable NetWare	NetWare Lite
DISABLE LOGIN	X	X		
DISABLE TRANSACTIONS	X			
DISABLE TTS		X		
DISK	X			
DISMOUNT	X	X		
DOWN	X	X		
REMOVE	X	X	X	
DOS	X			
ENABLE LOGIN		X		X
ENABLE TRANSACTIONS	X			
ENABLE TTS		X		
LOAD		X		
REMIRROR		X		
RESET ROUTER	X	X		
SECURE CONSOLE		X		
SET		X		
SET TIME	X	X		
SET TIMEZONE			X	
SETTTS	X	X		
TRACK ON/OFF	X	X	X	
UNBIND		X		
UNLOAD		X		
UNMIRROR	X			
UPGRADE		X		
UPS TIME		X		
VREPAIR	X	X		
WSUPDATE	X	X		

	v2.2	v3.11	Portable NetWare	NetWare Lite
ZTEST	x			
Network Operations				
AUDIT				x
ATOTAL	x	x	x	
BREQUEST	x	x	x	
BROUTER	x	x		
BRQPARMS	x	x		
BSETUP	x	x		
BSPXCOM	x	x		
BTRIEVE	x	x		
CLIB		x		
COLORPAL	x	x	x	
DOSGEN	x	x	x	
FILER	x	x	x	
IPX			x	
IPXS		x		
MAKEUSER	x	x	x	
MATHLIB		x		
MATHLIBC		x		
ROUTE	x	x		
RSPX		x	x	
SCONSOLE			x	
SESSION	x	x	x	
SET		x		
STARTNW			x	
STOPNVT			x	
STOPNW			x	

	v2.2	v3.11	Portable NetWare	NetWare Lite
STREAMS		X		
SYSCON	X	X	X	
USERDEF	X	X	X	
Print Services				
CAPTURE	X	X	X	X
ENDCAP	X	X	X	
NPLIST				X
NPRINT	X	X	X	
PCONSOLE	X	X	X	
PRINT				X
PRINTCON	X	X	X	
PRINTDEF	X	X	X	
PRINTER	X			
PSC	X	X	X	
PSERVER	X	X	X	
PSTAT	X			
QUEUE	X			
RPRINTER	X	X	X	
SPOOL	X	X		
Router Resources				
CONFIG	X	X		
DOWN	X	X		
ECONFIG	X	X	X	
MONITOR	X	X		
OFF	X	X		
RESET ROUTER	X	X		
ROUTEGEN	X	X		
RROUTER			X	

	v2.2	v3.11	Portable NetWare	NetWare Lite
Screen Commands				
BROADCAST	X	X		
CASTOFF	X	X	X	
CASTON	X	X	X	
CLEAR MESSAGE	X			
CLS		X		
EXIT		X		
OFF	X	X		
RECEIVE				X
SEND	X	X	X	X
Security				
ALLOW		X	X	
FILER	X	X	X	
FLAG	X	X	X	
FLAGDIR	X	X	X	
GRANT	X	X	X	
HYBRID			X	
LISTDIR	X	X	X	
LOGIN	X	X	X	X
LOGOUT		X	X	X
REMOVE		X	X	
REVOKE		X	X	
RIGHTS	X	X	X	
SECURE CONSOLE		X		
SECURITY	X	X	X	
SETPASS	X	X	X	X
TLIST	X	X	X	

	v2.2	v3.11	Portable NetWare	NetWare Lite
Station Configuration				
ECONFIG	x	x	x	
ETHERRPL		x		
NVT			x	
PCN2RPL		x		
TOKENRPL		x		
User Identification				
LISTDIR	x	x	x	
SEND	x	x	x	x
ULIST				x
USERLIST	x	x	x	
WHOAMI	x	x	x	
Volume/Directory Management				
DSPACE		x		
LISTDIR	x	x	x	
MAP	x	x	x	
RENDIR	x	x	x	
SETDIR			x	
VOLINFO	x	x	x	

APPENDIX D

ISO/OSI-Compatible Standards and Protocols

The ISO/OSI Reference Model is a seven-layer model for data communications, defined in International Organization for Standardization (ISO) standard 7498. Message packets are designed to carry both data and information that moves them from layer to layer. For example, Figure 1 (on the following page) shows the flow of a message, such as a word processing document, from a Client station's Application (Layer 7). It is provided with information as it moves through Presentation (Layer 6), Session (Layer 5), Transport (Layer 4), Network (Layer 3), Data link (Layer 2), and the Physical Layer (Layer 1). At this point, the message is moved by cable or other means to the Server, where it moves from Layer 1 to Layer 7, transmission information being removed at each layer. When the message reaches the Server station's Application Layer, it is in the form originated at the Client station.

Portions of the Reference Model have been implemented by three types of standards and protocols. **Media Access Protocols** for network topology and transmission access cover the Physical and Data Link layers. They include ARCnet (Datapoint Corp.), Ethernet and CSMA/CD (IEEE 802.3), Ethernet II (Xerox), high-level data link control (CCITT X.25), token bus (IEEE 802.4), and token ring (IEEE 802.5). CSMA/CD, token bus, and token ring are among the protocols included in the U.S. government's GOSIP (Government Open Systems Interconnection Profile).

NetWare's Open Data-Link Interface (ODI) is an example of the transition from Media Access Protocols to the **Transport Protocols** that comprise the Network and Transport layers. The **Service Protocols** make up Layer 5, the Session Layer, Layer 6, Presentation, and Layer 7, Application. Transport and service protocols available to NetWare users include AppleTalk (Apple Computer), IPX/SPX (Novell), Systems Network Architecture (IBM), and TCP/IP. Layer 7 includes file transfer, electronic mail (CCITT X.500), messages (CCITT X.400), and print job transfer.

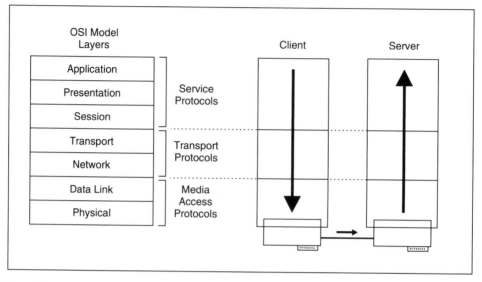

Figure 1: The flow of a message from a Client's station to the Server.

APPENDIX E

Resources

Magazines:

LAN Times
Mc-Graw Hill Inc.
7050 Union Park Center, Suite 240
Midvale, Utah 84047
801/565-1060

Network Computing
CMP Publication, Inc.
600 Community Drive
Manhasset, NY 11030
516/562-5071

Data Communications
McGraw-Hill Inc.
McGraw-Hill Building
1221 Avenue of the Americas
New York, NY 10020
212/512-2000

Books:

IEEE Standard Dictionary of Electrical and Electronics Terms, current edition (New York: Institute of Electrical and Electronics Engineers).

John E. McNamara. *Technical Aspects of Data Communication*, 3rd ed. (Digital Press, 1988).

Andrew S. Tanenbaum. *Computer Networks* (Englewood Cliffs., NJ: Prentice-Hall, Inc., 1981).

Tracy L. MaQuey, ed. *The User's Directory of Computer Networks* (Digital Press, 1990).

Organizations:

*American National Standards
Institute (ANSI)*
1430 Broadway
New York, NY 10036

Electronic Industries Association
2001 Eye St., NW
Washington, DC 20006

*Institute of Electrical and
Electronics Engineers (IEEE)*
United Engineering Center
345 E. 47th St.
New York, NY 10017

*National Institute of Standards and
Technology (NIST)*
Bldg. 233
Gaithersburg, Md 20899

A Library of Technical References from M&T Books

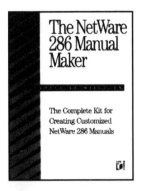

A Library of Technical References from M&T Books

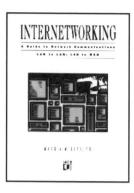

Internetworking
A Guide to Network Communications
LAN to LAN; LAN to WAN
by Mark A. Miller, P.E.

This book addresses all aspects of LAN and WAN (wide-area network) integrations, detailing the hardware, software, and communication products available. In-depth discussions describe the functions, design, and performance of repeaters, bridges, routers, and gateways. Communication facilities such as leased lines, T-1 circuits and access to packed switched public data networks (PSPDNs) are compared, helping LAN managers decide which is most viable for their internetwork. Also examined are the X.25, TCP/IP, and XNS protocols, as well as the internetworking capabilities and interoperability constraints of the most popular networks, including NetWare, LAN Server, 3+Open™, VINES®, and AppleTalk. 425 pp.

Book only   **Item #143-1**   **$34.95**

LAN Primer
An Introduction to Local Area Networks
by Greg Nunemacher

A complete introduction to local area networks (LANs), this book is a must for anyone who needs to know basic LAN principles. It includes a complete overview of LANs, clearly defining what a LAN is, the functions of a LAN, and how LANs fit into the field of telecommunications. The author discusses the specifics of building a LAN, including the required hardware and software, an overview of the types of products available, deciding what products to purchase, and assembling the pieces into a working LAN system. *LAN Primer* also includes case studies that illustrate how LAN principles work. Particular focus is given to Ethernet and Token-Ring. 221 pp.

Book only   **Item #127-X**   **$24.95**

Available at bookstores everywhere or call
1-800-533-4372 (in CA 1-800-356-2002)

ORDER FORM

To Order: Return this form with your payment to M&T books, 501 Galveston Drive, Redwood City, CA 94063 or **call toll-free 1-800-533-4372 (in California, call 1-800-356-2002).**

ITEM #	DESCRIPTION	DISK	PRICE

Subtotal _____

CA residents add sales tax ____% _____

Add $3.75 per item for shipping and handling _____

TOTAL _____

NOTE: **FREE SHIPPING** ON ORDERS OF THREE OR MORE BOOKS.

Charge my:

❏ **Visa**

❏ **MasterCard**

❏ **AmExpress**

❏ **Check enclosed, payable to M&T Books.**

CARD NO. _____

SIGNATURE _____ EXP. DATE _____

NAME _____

ADDRESS _____

CITY _____

STATE _____ ZIP _____

M&T GUARANTEE: If your are not satisfied with your order for any reason, return it to us within 25 days of receipt for a full refund. Note: Refunds on disks apply only when returned with book within guarantee period. Disks damaged in transit or defective will be promptly replaced, but cannot be exchanged for a disk from a different title.

8059

1-800-533-4372 (in CA 1-800-356-2002)